THE KITCHEN GARDEN

Keith Mossman

Keith Mossman was born in 1913, into
a farming family. He studied horticulture
and agriculture, and has spent most of
his life close to the soil. He has had
wide experience with private gardens,
and for ten years managed a market
garden single-handed. He is a freelance
journalist and has had two works
published on horticulture and gardening.
He is now retired and lives in Essex.

The Kitchen Garden

KEITH MOSSMAN

SPHERE BOOKS LIMITED
30/32 Gray's Inn Road, London, WC1X 8JL

First published in Great Britain in 1972
by Sphere Books Ltd.
© Keith Mossman, 1972

TRADE
MARK

Set in Monotype Garamond

Printed in Great Britain by
Hazell Watson & Viney Ltd,
Aylesbury, Bucks

Contents

Introduction

Fruit and vegetables from the garden are always welcome. Cost, freshness and quality are usually in their favour as compared with the purchased product, and every true gardener knows that the description 'home-grown' makes any item on the menu taste better.

Yet the reasons for growing things to eat instead of to look at are not merely economic or dietetic. This is a book for gardeners, however limited their field of operations may seem to be, and it is as gardeners that we should consider the possibilities.

Maybe the pendulum has swung too far from the utilitarian to the purely decorative, and the time has come to restore the balance. Of all hobbies gardening is the most infinitely versatile, it can fit all tastes and ages, be compressed or expanded, cost the earth or run happily on a shoestring. The thing to bear in mind is there is never just *one* sort of gardening to which one has to stick—that as things have been they remain. To accept that is to give up most of the fun.

So—with the revival of interest in home cookery can we not have a matching interest in home growing? Let's have the kitchen garden back again; and with it some of the enterprise and experimental zeal that has returned to the kitchen. Not the dull repetition of the same old vegetables on their segregated patch, but new varieties, decorative in themselves or combined with decorative schemes. Little fruit trees instead of flowering shrubs, bare walls clad with the fruiting vine, courtyard and patio gay with tomato and strawberry as a change from the scarlet of geranium. There's nothing impracticable about any of this, more and more ordinary gardeners are finding pleasure and interest in such ideas.

We are writing for gardeners in towns and some of them, especially those with very small plots in older built-up areas, have their particular problems. The worst of these, nine times out of ten, is an utterly worn-out soil, and to this we give a good deal of attention. In some ways the outlook for urban gardeners has improved; the clean air acts have made all the difference to the quality of light in the larger cities. On many a London roof garden light intensity is as good as in the country. The rain too is cleaner and no longer loaded with harmful acids.

Some advantages the town gardener has always possessed. Bird damage is less than in the country, so is infestation by air-borne weed seeds. Above all, the climate is milder; winter nights are warmer, and destructive spring frosts almost unknown, in city areas.

If your location is so urban that you have no garden plot at all you may still use whatever open space you *do* have. That is to say you can grow top fruits, strawberries, salads, herbs, mushrooms. . . . Surely enough to be going on with?

CHAPTER ONE

Ways and Means

THE SOIL

COMPOST

OTHER ORGANIC MANURES

GARDEN LAYOUT

GARDENING GUIDE

GARDENING GLOSSARY

Ways and Means

Gardening is by far the most popular outdoor hobby in this country. Its appeal is based on the great diversity of interests and opportunities which it offers, and also, perhaps, on the innumerable difficulties and obstacles which seem to be an integral part of any really satisfying activity. Sometimes, indeed, the difficulties and failures loom larger than the positive results, and one may be tempted to 'pack it in'. And then one reads the new seed catalogues and hope springs eternal.

For you, the town gardener anxious to vary the routine, to cut lettuces instead of the lawn and to match the bunch of June roses with the dish of June strawberries, there are obstacles in plenty. Best begin, then, by admitting their existence and looking for ways round them.

The truth is—though few believe it—that the small garden producing a succession of edible crops is a better proof of horticultural skill than the one which is merely lovely to look at. After all, the chap with a fat wallet can load up his car at the garden centre with containerized plants of every description in full bloom, wallop them in the ground in total ignorance of their needs and habits, and in half an hour have a show like the centre-spread of a gardening magazine. But he could still be incapable of growing an eatable radish. Fortunately, the cult of instant gardening is confined to the decorative side, the kitchen gardener still has to know some good old-fashioned do-it-yourself horticulture.

A minor obstacle to the absolute novice is the way in which gardening writers always assume that he understands their language. For his benefit the chapter includes some elementary explanations.

Two real problems for the town food-grower are the state of his soil and the lack of space. Soils usually get worse as one progresses from the newer suburbs to the older city centres, and the most common complaint is that the garden won't grow anything because the soil is sour. Now 'sour' has a precise meaning—that the soil is acid, lacking in calcium, and needs liming. This may sometimes be the case, especially in industrial areas. But very often the poor, green-scummy, useless stuff is not 'sour'—it's dead. It has died of malnutrition, and corpse-reviver sprinkled from a packet will not be enough to bring it back to life. Tackle that problem effectively, though, and the smallest garden becomes a source of pleasure and profit.

As to lack of space, we shall consider ways of using what you have to the best advantage. As a gardening nation we are shockingly bad at that.

THE SOIL

The plant life of our planet depends upon the top six inches or so of the Earth's crust. Animal life depends upon the plants, which alone can build up simple chemicals into organic compounds. Destroy that infinitely thin skin of soil and human technology could not replace it; along with most advanced forms we should cease to exist.

Anyone who works with the soil has at least a subconscious feeling of this vital importance, but very rarely do we stop to ask ourselves what soil actually *is*. To ask ourselves that might sometimes be useful in a practical way, enabling us to make sounder decisions in dealing with the most valuable, and one of the most complex, substances on Earth.

It began as bits of primeval rock, broken down smaller and smaller by climatic and geological forces. The finest particles became clay and coarser ones sand; both contain minerals essential to plant life, but in their pure state neither will grow plants. Then very primitive algae and mosses began to appear, absorbing carbon dioxide from the atmosphere and building carbon compounds in their tissues. They died and decayed, and slowly their rotting substance mingled with the pulverized rocks to form a mixture into which more complex plants would eventually thrust down roots, extract food materials, and in their turn die and add their slowly oxidizing remains to the soil layer that was in process of creation.

This accumulating organic matter ('organic' means simply that which is, or once was, alive) is what we call humus. Its structure and functions are complicated but we may say that basically it makes the difference between fertile soil and sterile desert.

The accretion of humus is a continuous process in nature. Every leaf that falls, every insect that dies in the soil, contributes to the credit side of the balance. Left to herself Nature never overdraws on the account. Man, unfortunately, often does.

We may not appreciate the gradual build-up of fertility, but there is no excuse for not seeing what happens when it is squandered. North Africa was not always the desert that the Eighth Army knew, it was once a great farming area of the Roman Empire. It was overcropped, nothing was paid back, its fertility was exported and went down the sewers of Rome and its soil died. The American plains had thousands of years of grass and grazing bison in their account. They were ploughed up to grow corn for Europe and dosed with chemical fertilizers when yields began to fall. But the humus reserves had been spent and much of the good dark loam had become loose dust. In sun and wind the soil took to the air and thousands of ruined farmers took to the roads.

Is this irrelevant to one's own pocket-handkerchief of ground? I think not, for soil, like peace, is indivisible. What is bad for 1,000 acres is bad for 10 sq. yds. In the long run the right results are not achieved by the use of the wrong methods, and 'wrong' here means technically, not morally, wrong.

The trouble is that we like things simple. When it was proved that plants need nitrogen, phosphorous and potassium to make them flourish it seemed obvious that by applying these elements as soluble compounds the tedious processes that produce them naturally in the soil would be by-passed. Then it was found that the elements boron, manganese, zinc, iron, magnesium, copper and molybdenum were also necessary in minute quantities and had always been provided by organic manures. But even with the addition of these trace elements chemical fertilizers suffer from a basic deficiency. They are designed to feed a particular crop; organic manures feed the soil, and a well-fed soil means that you can stop worrying about the individual manurial requirement of everything you grow.

The phrase 'the living soil' is not poetic exaggeration. A teaspoonful of fertile soil is supposed to contain more microscopic creatures than there are human beings on Earth. Never having counted them I wouldn't know, but they have to be fed if the soil is to remain productive, and they can no more live on chemicals than you can.

Given the materials to consume—the stuff we call 'manure' or 'compost'—this teeming population enters into an active partnership with the growing plant to provide the intricate balance of chemicals for its roots to absorb. It also converts the manures into humus and maintains the soil structure.

This concept of 'structure' is hard to define, yet every experienced gardener knows what it means. A good soil has certain *physical* characteristics which are not revealed by chemical analysis. It is sufficiently open in texture for roots to penetrate easily and for a myriad pockets of air to exist; soil without oxygen will grow nothing. Like a soft sponge it will hold water without becoming waterlogged and its surface will be easily workable. If you tread on the wet surface of a clay soil your footprint will dry in the sun to something like a brick. But fork compost or peat into the top few inches and the surface will not be compacted and made unworkable in this way. A heavy soil without enough organic material is cold and sticky and root systems are slow to develop in it. Light soils with the same deficiency cannot retain moisture. In both cases plants will go hungry on inorganic fertilizers.

We have spent rather long on this subject—which may look somewhat theoretical for a purely practical little book— because you will want to know why this insistence all through on organic methods. It isn't theoretical at all, and it has nothing to do with muck, magic, and dancing round the maypole. The hard facts are that a lot of townspeople with tiny gardens are keen on growing something good to eat but get poor results despite all the glossy know-how of the gardening press. There may be many secondary reasons for this, air pollution, toxic industrial wastes in rainfall, lack of sunlight, and so on. But I'm afraid the basic long-term reason is simple. Since the disappearance of the horse town soils have fared worse than country ones.

About 1900 the system of French Gardening was brought to England from the market gardens of Paris, where it was said that the top practitioners could grow melons on the pavement. They created their own black soil, the *terreau*, by using vast quantities of horse manure; from quite small areas the quantity and quality of their produce gave France a gastronomic reputation by no means due solely to her cooks.

When French Gardening was demonstrated here the instructors asked for 1,200 tons of manure to the acre. This is about 1 ton to every 4 sq. yds., which none of us could now obtain or afford, or would know how to deal with. But the needs of fruit, vegetable, and salad crops are the same now as they were then, and to succeed with them the same principles apply.

Town gardens have suffered both from lack of organic manures and from over-use of artificials, which has often worsened the situation by oxydizing the remaining humus, breaking down the soil structure and reducing the earthworm and bacterial populations. And all the time the materials that could put things right are being consigned to the bonfire and the dustbin.

COMPOST

The word has two meanings; here it means decomposing wastes used for feeding the soil, in another context it is a specially-prepared material for growing plants in pots and other containers.

Compost-making has acquired such an elaborate mystique that some gardeners have come to feel that they ought to have a degree in biochemistry or be an ordained priest before attempting it. In essence nothing could be simpler. I remember as a boy finding an abandoned haystack on my uncle's farm—it had been of such poor quality as not to justify the expense of thatching. Now it was grey on the outside and black within. It had shrunk to a fraction of its original size; blackberry growths from the hedge had layered themselves in it, sending clean white roots through the friable material; colonies of lively red worms spilled out as I investigated. It was a great heap of compost, and apart from the initial building of the stack nobody had 'made' it.

Building The Heap. In the small garden some sort of surround is needed to keep it tidy. Compost bins can be bought but are no better than the home-made job.

Drive four wooden posts into the ground to form a square with 4 ft. sides; their height above ground should be at least 3 ft. Enclose three sides of the square with horizontal wooden slats (old packing-case boards or any stout timber will do) with a 1 in. space between. Make a removable slatted frame to fit the fourth side.

Double compost bin. Front of right-hand one removed to take out compost

Weldmesh or chain-link fencing can be used instead of timber slats, but not wire netting which bulges and rapidly corrodes. The sides must not be solid because air must have free access to the heap. If two of these slatted bins can be made side by side in 'semi-detached' form it is possible to organize a more continuous supply of compost, with one lot maturing and being used while the neighbouring heap is building up. The second bin will of course require only two more corner posts.

The bottom of the bin must be of bare ground, weed-free if possible, to permit drainage and the entry of earthworms into the heap. The movable side, intended to make the removal of finished compost easier, is fastened in place. Operations are best started in spring, when the main supply of material is about to become available.

Compost heaps need not be turned, as most gardeners who are short of time have found out for themselves. The outside of the heap will not be properly decomposed but is used to form part of the succeeding heap when the compost is used. The more material that can be put into the bin at a time, the better. A good depth of waste will heat up with decomposition, destroying weed seeds and roots and hastening the composting process. The end result will be the same, though, if it has to be 'little and often', which is more probable in the small garden.

Material added to the bin must be moist, the essential breaking-down action cannot take place in the dry. Sprinkle each layer with water as it is added unless it is actually raining. The contents of the bin will keep on sinking as fast as you add to them, but when the top of the bin is reached and the shrinkage seems to have stopped, cover the half-made compost with a sheet of polythene held down with bricks or soil. This helps to keep some warmth in and prevent it becoming too wet during the later stages.

The Raw Materials. Dr. W. E. Shewell-Cooper, in referring to the humus deficiency of town gardens, maintains that the keen vegetable grower must promise never to make a bonfire, and that the women of the household must get used to putting the tea leaves and fruit and vegetable peels on the compost instead of in the dustbin.

With the exception of wood, leather and bones most organic substances can be composted. Lawn mowings, weeds, crop residues (bean tops, etc.), dead flowers and bedding plants, leaves and trimmings from bought vegetables, manure from poultry, rabbits, or pigeons, and crops grown specially for the purpose.

Cotton and woollen rags can go on, but not nylon or other synthetic fibres. Paper rots down satisfactorily if torn up and thoroughly soaked; I remember putting down paper sacks on which to stand up-ended cloches which were out of use and finding at the end of a wet summer that not a trace of the tough paper remained—the worms had taken it below and were composting it in their own way. Straw is good, but without the admixture of animal manures is slow in becoming usable. To anyone able to get straw bales I would suggest building the compost bin with them. They hold the heap together for a year and are then broken up sufficiently rotted to go into a new heap or for use as a mulch. Admittedly straw bales are not easy to get in town, but anyone with a car who takes a run in the country in August and September with an eye open for harvesting operations can usually find a farmer willing to load roof rack and boot with as many as you can take.

If you have non-composting neighbours a few large polythene bags might be handed around with the request that weeds and lawn mowings be dropped over your fence. An occasional fresh lettuce in the other direction will help to maintain the supply. More ambitiously, you might emulate an enthusiastic food-grower of my acquaintance who collects a car-load of vegetable waste from local greengrocers on Saturday mornings. Quick-growing crops like mustard are

17

often sown on vacant ground and dug in as 'green manure', but better results may be obtained by pulling the green manure up and composting it, rather than compelling the soil bacteria to deal with it in the raw state. Interesting results are being obtained in the making of compost from the perennial comfrey, which produces great quantities of foliage rich in potash and other vital foods.

Cabbage stalks and other hard vegetable matter should be chopped up before being added to the heap. The American gardener has a range of mechanical shredders available for this sort of thing, but for most materials the exercise is pointless.

Don't include woody hedge trimmings or rose prunings. Don't add too many dead leaves in autumn, their decomposition is very slow and they should be well mixed with more sappy things. Don't add food scraps or things like fish-heads, which may attract rats and mice and will probably smell. Well-managed compost, kept properly moist and exposed to air, will be no nuisance to you or to your neighbours—much less so than the average sodden pile of mixed rubbish, waiting to be burned.

Activators. Many types of activator are on offer, ranging from herbal mixtures to proprietary chemicals, but none is essential. There's nothing more certain than that everything once living will ultimately decay and that at the right stage of the process will enrich the soil. Use of an activator may, however, speed things up and improve the final product.

Sir Albert Howard's 'Indore' method uses animal manures in alternate layers with vegetable wastes, but this is usually out of the question. Possible alternatives are municipal compost or processed sludge, applied in 1 in. layers to every 1 ft. of greenstuff, but the handiest activator is probably fish meal. This is a valuable concentrated organic for general use in small quantities, and if a dusting of 4 ozs. is applied to our compost bin for every foot of raw material and a very occasional sprinkle of hydrated lime is also added, no other activator is needed.

Using the Compost. It is ready for use when the interior of the heap has rotted to a loose, dark brown substance with a rather pleasant earthy smell. This may take up to 6 months, hence the advisability of having two heaps on the go.

Dig it in at any time of year, or use it as a mulch between

growing crops to be dug in later. Aim at making enough for at least a large bucketful per sq. yd. Unlike inorganic fertilizers you cannot use too much.

A 4 by 4 ft. bin half-full of finished compost will contain 3 to 4 cwts. If you go to a garden shop and buy a decorative bag of composted horse manure it will cost you £1·30 for 56 lb. The actual cash value of home-made compost can hardly be evaluated, but its qualities in the standard fertilizer terms of nitrogen, phosphoric acid and potash have been tested many times. Analyses by the Henry Doubleday Research Association, which is concerned with the experiments on comfrey mentioned above, have given comparative figures for farmyard manure and various samples of compost. The relevant nitrogen figures show percentages of 2·2 for farmyard manure and from 1·3 to 4·45 for the composts; of phosphorous, 1·05 for FYM and between 0·6 and 1·95 for the composts, and of potash 2·0 for FYM and from 0·3 to 5·3 for the composts. The lower compost figures are all for the municipal, not the home-made, product. So even in the main growth elements compost can hold its own, and this is to disregard its long-term cumulative benefit to the soil.

OTHER ORGANIC MANURES

These may be purchased to supplement supplies of compost, or for use before it becomes available. Some are bulky and add substantially to the humus content. Others are as concentrated and easy to handle as inorganics. All are more or less expensive, and the less you depend on them the better for your pocket.

Farmyard Manure. An expensive rarity. Stable manure may be available if you live near a riding school or similar establishment but will probably be too fresh and strawy for immediate use. Best incorporated in the compost heap. The same applies to poultry manure from battery or deep litter plants, and I would in any case be wary of these because of their pervasive smell. Be wary too of the smart lad in a plain van who offers you 'genuine farm manure' by the bag; strange stories circulate about the contents of the bags when examined. The proprietary composted manures such as D.O.D. or 6X. are very good if you can afford them.

Sedge Peat. A most valuable source of humus to help out

the supply of compost. Although usually described as a soil conditioner it is also a source of plant food as it decays. Dig it in or use it as a mulch between growing crops. Up to a bucketful per sq. yd. applied at any time of the year will improve both heavy and light lands. There is no fear of applications at this rate making any normal soil too acid.

Sedge peat is better value than sphagnum peat, and a cwt. bale is a cheaper way of buying than small bags. Don't occupy precious shed space with the bale, let it lie outside exposed to the elements. Peat usually comes too dry and the bale may be hard to break up; rain soaks it and frost loosens it, making it just right to handle.

Municipal Compost and Sludge. Sounds unattractive, but this type of product made by local authorities is not to be despised. As we have seen, it is not as good as home-produced compost, but is convenient in use and the processed sludge can be used as a top-dressing and forked in as easily as fertilizer. Only a tiny minority of councils turn their wastes and sewage residues into this useful product instead of polluting land and water with them and they should be encouraged. To find out if you can obtain it locally enquire at the Borough Surveyor's office. If the answer is 'No' express strong disapproval.

Hop Manure. Always a favourite with amateur gardeners but I doubt if its superiority over peat justifies the difference in price. Peat, reinforced with fish meal at 3 oz. to the pailful would be as good and cheaper.

Fish Meal or Fish Manure. This is a concentrated organic fertilizer, used as a compost activator or in small quantities as a quick-acting plant food. All fish manures are strong in nitrogen and the best are also rich in potash. Those with a high potash analysis are worth the little extra cost. You need not fear a fishy taint in crops grown with the stuff, market gardeners with a reputation to lose have been using it for the last 100 years.

Bone Meal. A source of phosphates, but it releases them only very slowly. The more finely ground it is the quicker the phosphates become available, and the finest of all, steamed bone flour, is the one to use in making up potting composts for things like tomatoes or fruit trees in pots. When planting fruit trees or soft fruits in the open use two or three good handfuls of a coarser grade at each station or for each yard run.

Dried Blood. This is powerfully nitrogenous and a real growth promoter. Unfortunately it is now too expensive for general use, but might occasionally be justified on leafy things like brassicas and spinach. I wouldn't use dried blood on pot plants in or near the house—it sometimes draws attention to itself, especially in hot weather.

Hoof and Horn. Although slower in action than dried blood this too is basically a nitrogenous organic. It is fairly long lasting and useful in potting composts, being a standard ingredient of JI potting.

A balanced mixture of these manufactured organics, Blood, Fish and Bone Fertilizer, is sold by Woodmans of Pinner.

Liquid Manures. Some are genuinely organic preparations, others are said to have an organic base, which may mean anything. Plants can only assimilate nutrients in liquid form, so a liquid food is much more quickly taken up than a dry substance which has first to be dissolved by the soil moisture. Never try to improve things by making a stronger brew than the makers advise. A safer rule is 'take more water with it' and give them a longer drink. A gallon once a week, for instance, for every 2 ft. of runner bean row and each outdoor tomato plant in full bearing.

Wood Ashes. One excuse for the bonfire is that 'wood ashes are so good—full of potash, you know'. The real reason for bonfires, I suspect, is that most of us are incipient pyromaniacs. Muddling about with the things is more fun than organizing a compost heap, at least until the results of compost become apparent. Of course burnt vegetable matter contains potash, but the burning didn't create it. It was there all the time, along with a lot of other things which have now gone up in smoke.

So burn only woody materials, and get the ashes into the ground before the soluble potash is leached out by rain.

Lime. Soils may be acid or alkaline or neutral. You will often see this expressed as a pH number; pH 7 is neutral, above pH 7 is alkaline, below is acid. Unless you go in for soil testing or have an analysis done (get the address of the Horticultural Adviser from the local library if you want one) you needn't worry about the actual figures. Most food crops like it slightly acid, about pH 6·5, except for legumes and brassicas. In practical terms this means a light dressing of hydrated lime on ground intended for these crops even though this is unnecessary for others.

Most organically fed soils maintain a reasonable balance, depending on the natural supplies of calcium. Very chalky soils require a lot of humus to reduce their alkalinity, and they positively eat up organic manures. Heavy soils often have a chalk subsoil and will need only an occasional liming. Peaty and sandy soils can probably do with a 4 oz. per sq. yd. dose of ground limestone or hydrated lime every other year. Don't buy quicklime, it's nasty stuff to handle and has no advantages.

GARDEN LAYOUT

Unless you are lucky enough to be starting from scratch, or are one of those ruthless types, there may be no fundamental garden planning open to you. But looking around one does see many missed opportunities.

Any true gardener will be concerned about the *appearance* of his garden. To be reading this book he must also be wanting something more than aesthetic satisfaction from it; he wants fresh food. Can he get the one without sacrificing the other?

The basic shape of the town garden, be it old urban or new suburban, is a rectangular plot with the dwelling house near one end of the rectangle. There may or may not be an ornamental area in front of the house and the back garden is likely to consist of lawn and flower bed near the house and a kitchen garden section at the further end. This pattern will vary with the size of the plot, but it is the typical outline.

A view of the 'business end' of these gardens as one approaches a city by rail is often depressing. Half-hearted cultivation, wasted space, weed-grown corners, disorderly piles of junk, bean poles waving drunkenly in the winter winds, bare fences where fruit would grow, even precious equipment like greenhouses and frames standing desolate and unused. No wonder the growing of edible crops is thought to 'make the place untidy'.

Many people, of course, keep both the ornamental and utility sections looking attractive, and divide them by ingenious forms of screening. But a radically different approach is necessary if one wants worthwhile additions to the menu from the very small garden.

To combine these different functions we need to go back to a neglected tradition and treat them the same. The Saxons grew the vegetables in a 'wort yard' and their roses and other native flowers with them. (The word 'yard' for garden has survived across the Atlantic; I remember being momentarily puzzled when the American tenant of an East Anglian cottage told me that he had 'spaded over the yard in the Fall'). The mediaeval monk drew no line between the eatable, the herb and the flower—why should he since all reflected God's care for different aspects of man's being?

With the great era of landscaping the gentry wanted their houses surrounded by parkland. The kitchen gardens were pushed out of sight, sometimes to a quarter of a mile away, and this separation became general except in cottage gardens.

The rural worker's garden, though a lot bigger than that of the modern townsman, had no room for complete separation and he hadn't much spare energy for flower growing. Yet such cottage gardens were often attractive in appearance and rarely lacked colour and scent. One which sticks in my memory was an almost perfect square, bisected by a straight cobbled path. Both halves were vegetable plots, tidy and well-filled. Along the edges of these plots, forming a continuous avenue along both sides of the path, were standard rose trees, almost touching and in full bloom. I learnt later that they were home-budded on briar stock dug from the hedgerows. The whole effect was visually satisfying in its simplicity, yet it could easily have been just another mucky bit of kitchen garden.

It's not for me to draw elaborate plans for *your* garden—after all, you know it and I don't—but I'm sure you can replace ornamental plantings with fruit and vegetables without spoiling the look of it. You may grow them separately or together, and the book suggests edible crops which are decorative in themselves. First, though, there are a few general rules to be observed, and some questions to be put.

When a crop is finished don't leave its remains in the ground. Things like brassica stumps and bolted lettuce should go straight to the compost heap and their place be dug or mulched or replanted. The thing to avoid is a *neglected* look.

The same applies to equipment. Keep greenhouse or frame in repair with the glass clean and broken panes replaced. Cloches when out of use should be nested together standing on end on a strip of black polythene to stop weeds growing up between them. Don't leave them scattered around to get broken.

Supports for climbing crops like runner beans, squashes and cucumbers should be made a little more substantial than you really think necessary; a partial collapse looks terrible and a complete one ruins the crop.

Plan the use of light. The very small garden, fenced and surrounded by buildings, may get plenty of sunlight at mid-summer but very little in the winter. The sun is not only low in the sky then but its arc is much shorter, so that you get hardly any sunshine from east or west. There may be only one spot reached by it all the year round and that is the place for any winter crops under cloches.

Use imagination and forget conventions. If a small flower bed near the house needs a border planting, why not parsley? If a row of calabresse looks dull in a place where you formerly grew something colourful, plant two or three cactus dahlias in the row; they will blend with the light green of the calabresse and finish at the same time. This sort of experimentation may not always succeed, but the spice of something different improves any hobby.

You may have only a courtyard or a patio. If so, Chapter 6 is intended for you. Just now we are dealing with an actual garden, though you may think it too small to be much use. Lack of space, or just unwillingness to have a bash?

Is there a space of south-facing wall on the house large enough to take a fan-trained peach? Or facing north to take a Morello cherry, or between two windows to take a cordon pear, or below a ground floor window to take cordon red currants or gooseberries? Or a sheltered angle just right for grapevine?

What about that shady strip alongside the fence where nothing seems to do well? Raspberries will fruit and ripen in shade given manure or compost.

Did you once think of planting an ornamental tree on the lawn? Why not a Family apple tree, which will give you at least three different varieties in a very small space.

That weedy corner where you run the wheelbarrow when you're not using it. Ever thought of up-ending the barrow against the fence, slaughtering the weeds and planting a couple of rhubarb crowns?

Why waste time clipping that pointless bit of shrubbery where the path changes direction? Have it out and substitute globe artichokes, they look magnificent in summer and the ground can be planted with crocuses which finish blooming before they reappear in the spring.

The washing-line post (yes, they still exist, launderettes notwithstanding), could it be disguised cheaply? It certainly can for part of the year if you cultivate round its base, run strings from the top maypole-wise, and sow a circle of runner beans.

The mixed border that looks on its last legs, with eel-wormy phlox and weed-ridden Mrs. Sinkins, for how long have you been vowing to scrap it and start afresh? So how about manuring it well and growing vegetables for a year or two before replanting in clean good soil?

Look around, and note how many questions of this sort come to mind. Affirmative answers? You'll be surprised.

GARDENING GUIDE

Things which the expert takes for granted are often far from obvious to the beginner. These tips are for the latter; the expert can ignore them.

One nearly always has to begin by buying tools, plants and seeds, and this should never be done hurriedly or on the basis of an exciting advertisement that catches your eye. Most gardening operations are simple and easily mastered, but all of them need a little practice, and buying just what you require is no exception. So make at least an outline plan of your garden's future development, and avoid buying anything that the plan doesn't need or that you cannot handle. If in doubt as to varieties or quantities explain the situation to your chosen supplier—he wants a satisfied customer.

Buying Bushes and Trees. Visit nurseries during the cropping season. Send for catalogues in the summer and order early. If trees or bushes cannot be planted immediately on delivery, the roots can be unwrapped and covered in a temporary trench ('heeling in'), or kept moist in a frost-proof shed. *Never allow dormant trees to remain wrapped up in a centrally heated house,* even for a few days.

When ordering grape vines or fig trees in pots, find out if they are going to be despatched in their containers or knocked out to reduce transport charges. It is sometimes worth paying a little extra to have them left in the pots if you are uncertain when planting will be possible.

Buying Seeds. Consult more than one catalogue if you are sending away for them and again order early, soon after Christmas if possible. Don't always choose the newest varieties, however gorgeous the descriptions and mouth-watering the pictures, let other people try them out. Any variety followed by the letters A.M. R.H.S. or H.C. R.H.S. has received an Award of Merit or a Highly Commended in Royal Horticultural Society trials and is good of its type.

Pelletted seed is a commercial development now available to the amateur. Small seeds are enclosed in protective coatings, making them larger, easier to sow thinly, and reducing waste and time spent in thinning. Fewer actual seeds per packet is another advantage—small gardeners usually get more than they can use. Pelletted seeds must have plenty of moisture for germination.

Never sow old seed with the possible exception of the brassicas, which will keep for up to three years. This warning does not necessarily apply to seeds in the special sealed packs introduced by Messrs Suttons, these may keep for more than one season *if the packet is unopened.*

Buying Tools and Sundries. Tools are expensive and if you have to buy the best rule is 'few and good'. The ideal digging tool is the stainless steel spade, preferably with a small (9 by 6 in.) blade. The small border fork is handier than the full size digging fork. A draw hoe is the best choice for weed control because of its use in taking out seed drills. The short-handled onion hoe is a wonderful weeding tool for those who like to get down on their knees—a position in which, according to Kipling, half a proper gardener's work is done. A rake and a pair of secateurs are essential, so is a length of hose and/or a watering can. A stainless steel trowel is a better buy than a cheaper trowel and hand fork, it does the work of both. It also replaces the dibber, used for planting; where not many plants are involved the trowel makes for better planting. The age-old advice to clean and oil tools after use is a counsel of perfection and safely ignored with stainless steel which may be put away dirty and brushed clean when dry. Add to the list a garden line—two pegs and a length of string—and a two gallon bucket, and that's enough to be going on with.

'Sundries' includes organic fertilizers like fish- and bone-meal, which should be bought in smallish quantities and stored dry and mouse-proof. Pots, containers and seed boxes are now usually in plastic, which is relatively cheap, light and long-lasting. For raising vegetable plants like marrows and tomatoes the peat pot which is itself planted is preferred. Soil-less composts of the Levington variety will keep, but the John Innes range is best bought as required and used fresh.

Cloche Management. The growers barn is the most popular and economical size of glass cloche; the low barn covers the same area and is suitable for low-growing things like lettuces but not for bush tomatoes or strawberries. Cloches are a valuable and adaptable form of protection and it should be possible to keep them almost continually in use. Always keep the glass clean and wash off any green algal deposit with detergent and a soft brush. In early spring, place cloches in position at least a week before sowing or planting under them. Have the ground perfectly level or the cloches will not join up accurately, if the roof glass of one gets just over or under that of its neighbour there may be a breakage on moving. Ventilate when neccessary by spacing $\frac{1}{2}$ in. apart, always keep ends in position.

In summer, cloched crops may need light shading. Smear the glass with limewash (a handful of hydrated lime to a quart of water; don't use a household distemper, it's too difficult to remove). Adequate moisture for cloche crops depends upon plenty of humus in the soil, allowing it to reach the roots by capillary action. But you will have to water most crops in the summer, and young seedlings with roots near the surface need frequent watering until established.

Plastic cloches are now available in variety. Some are made o, semi-rigid P.V.C. and the like, others of polythene on wire frames. Temperature under plastic tends to be lower than under glass and the latter is best for winter crops. Plastic cloches are vulnerable to high winds and you should make sure that any bought have some means of anchoring them to the ground.

Digging. Do it in the winter if possible, leaving the surface rough and exposed to frost (see 'Tilth' in the next section). For this reason I prefer the spade to the fork, which breaks up the soil. Double digging or trenching is now little practised, but the following version of it is worthwhile on the heavy

27

clays: Throw the spit well forward as you dig, leaving a space between the dug and undug. Then take the fork and drive it to its full depth repeatedly along the bottom of the trench so formed, lever the subsoil up and withdraw the fork, leaving the subsoil in position but now moved and broken all along the row. Revert to the spade and turn the topsoil onto it and repeat. This can make a great difference to root penetration and the vertical movement of moisture.

When digging in compost don't cram it in a solid wodge along the bottom of the trench, distribute it along the face of the dug portion so that it is spread throughout the topsoil. Lime should be applied to the surface after digging.

Hoeing and Weed Control. Frequent hoeing between rows is time well spent. Pull the draw hoe towards you with the edge of the blade just below the surface. This deals with both visible weeds and those already germinating below. Keep the hoe sharp by occasionally filing the edge. Leave weeds on the surface in dry weather, but rake them off for the compost heap when wet. The Dutch hoe, which is pushed instead of pulled, is preferred by some because the worker walks backwards and does not tread on the ground already hoed. Unfortunately it is no use for taking out seed drills.

One effect of hoeing is to produce a layer of loose soil sometimes called a 'soil mulch' from the way in which it preserves moisture. If two soil areas, one loose and friable and the other trodden down tight, are compared when the ground is drying out you will notice that the first gets the typically dry look while the second stays darker in colour with the moisture that is being drawn up and lost in evaporation.

Herbicides (the word means 'plant-killers') are a possible alternative to hoeing and hand weeding. The only one I would use is paraquat/diquat, marketed as Weedol. This is a contact poison which operates through the plants' foliage, not their roots. In the soil it breaks down and disappears. It can be applied from a watering can and will not harm crops provided it does not actually get onto their leaves or green stems. I find it very useful if a dense growth of annual weeds and grass has to be cleared quickly. It is also effective against many perennial weeds, though not, in my experience, against that universal plague, ground elder. But then there are only two things to be done about weeds of the ground elder calibre—you give up and leave them in possession or, as an old head gardener used to say, you 'never let them see a Sunday'. In other words you dig up as much as you can of every shoot that appears—every working day if need be.

Don't confuse Weedol with Weedex, the latter is a very persistent herbicide based on the chemical simazine which remains active in the top layer of soil.

For cleaning up weedy paths the best and cheapest weed-killer is still sodium chlorate, which is relatively non-toxic to all animals and birds. The only warning is that you don't let the kids start mixing it with caster sugar on the plea that they just want to make a little gunpowder. Too many have done it too successfully.

Pest Control. Fruit pests and diseases are dealt with briefly in the next chapter, but the subject does not get a lot of space among the cultural hints. The modern song-and-dance about it has given the impression that one must either engage in chemical warfare or give up gardening. The facts are:

(1) Well-grown crops have a natural resistance to enemies. Good cultivation is the best preventative.

(2) Superlative fruit and vegetables were grown in the past with the aid of very simple protective measures.

(3) The modern powerful insecticides are increasingly criticized. Aldrin and dieldrin are banned; the chlorinated hydrocarbons such as DDT and BHC are likely to be now that their ability to accumulate and persist in animal tissues is recognized. Malathion, a favourite with amateur gardeners, is similarly suspect. These pesticides are also proving counter-productive, killing off friendly predators like ladybirds and creating resistant strains of pests. We cannot go into this in detail—there is plenty of reading on the subject—but a voluntary resolve to use older and safer methods would in my opinion improve the whole standard of gardening.

(4) Safe and non-persistent pesticides, not chemically synthesized but derived from natural vegetable products, can now be bought everywhere.

The two best all-rounders are derris and pyrethrum. Some makers combine the two and they may be obtained in the usual forms of a liquid for making up your own spray or as aerosols. Cooper's Garden Aerosol is a good one. Derris is also widely used as a dust. Both are harmless to all warm-blooded life. Quassia and soap are still effective against aphis. The metaldehyde slug-killers are safe, but if possible should be covered with slightly-raised tiles or something similar to prevent them being eaten by birds and pets.

Hints on a few of the commoner worries:

Aphis. Spray as soon as detected. Pinch out tips of broad beans when enough pods are set, and of runner beans when top of supports is reached. These black fly spend the winter on Euonymous and Viburnum shrubs and if these are sprayed in March or April future trouble may be reduced. The grey cabbage aphis which attacks all brassicas should be sprayed with derris under the leaves and in crevices as soon as it appears. Many aphis colonies could be eliminated at the start by the pressure of finger and thumb, and even more by forceful spraying with pure water from a hose. Early observation is the prime need.

Caterpillars. Derris is effective as long as it makes contact with them. Look for the groups of eggs laid by cabbage white butterflies and burn them with the leaf. This species of caterpillar may be controlled by spraying with a solution of common salt, 2 oz. to a gallon of water, which doesn't hurt the plants.

Flea beetles on brassicas and radishes. Derris dust as soon as noticed. They are always worst on poor, dry soils.

Fruit pests. The practice of grease-banding fruit trees and spraying them with a tar-oil winter wash such as Mortegg is sound and safe, but if you have only one or two young trees are probably unneccessary. More about this at the end of Chapter 2.

Birds, bless their little hearts, can be extremely destructive. For the protection of seedlings black cotton is very effective when strung from pegs about 3 in. above the ground. I would emphasize that it must be *black*, its frightening effect depends on its invisibility. The house sparrow is the chief snapper-up of seedlings, but the greatest danger to soft fruit is the blackbird, though he is less of a menace in the town than in the country. Small-mesh netting, properly erected, is the only answer to him. The various bird repellants cannot be used on edible crops getting near harvesting because they work by making it taste nasty.

A few more nuisances, diseases as well as pests, will be noted as we go along, with suggested remedies based more on commonsense and 'plantsmanship' than on wonder drugs. Much research is going on in the natural control of plant ailments and enemies, and many old practices are being preached anew. Books and pamphlets are recommended for those interested.

Sowing. To germinate, a seed must have moisture, warmth, air, and a growing medium that its fragile root and shoot can penetrate. So—a good tilth, seeds not sown too deeply, or before the ground has warmed up, and if artificial watering is used to start germination this must be continued in dry weather until the seedlings are established. A seed which has sprouted and been allowed to dry out is finished.

Rake the soil surface level before sowing. Use a corner of the draw hoe to make a narrow drill and the full blade for a wide one. For the smallest seeds the drill should be little more than a deep scratch, for medium-sized ones like radish about and inch deep, and for beans not more than 2 in. Hold the hand close to the ground when sowing small seeds in windy weather, pull the soil back over the drill and tamp it down lightly with hoe or rake. Never attempt to sow in wet sticky ground.

If you are a non-stooper you could invest in a Wolf Sower, which is pushed along the drill by a long handle and does an even job. Sowing at stations and using pelleted seed simplify both sowing and thinning.

Sowing in the greenhouse; see Chapter 5.

GARDENING GLOSSARY

Every craft has its own special terms, and to know their exact meaning is useful when reading up the subject.

Here are some frequently-used bits of horticultural jargon.

ACTIVATOR. Material added to a compost heap to accelerate rotting-down process. Animal manures, fish meal, or proprietary product such as Fertosan.

AXIL. The angle formed by a branch or leaf-stalk and the stem. Laterals or side-shoots generally spring from the axils, and where not wanted, as in the tomato, should be rubbed out while small.

BLANCH. To make white by growing in darkness, as with celery, chicory, etc. This prevents the formation of green chlorophyll and of strong or bitter flavours. Successful blanching requires absolute darkness, even a chink of daylight can spoil the effect.

BOLT. To run to seed. When this happens prematurely, as it may do with lettuce, spinach, and other crops, the plants are useless. Poor dry soils are a major cause, and some varieties are more affected than others. Maintain soil humus and moisture and note non-bolting varieties in catalogues.

BREAK. To start into growth, as with a dormant bud on a branch which has been pruned back.

BROADCAST. To sow seed by scattering it over an area and raking it in, instead of sowing in a narrow trench or drill. Used for quick-growing things like radishes, but unsuitable for crops that must be spaced out and weeded.

CLONE. A word that turns up in fruit catalogues, e.g. 'A virus-free clone'. A plant propagated vegetatively, not by fertilized seed, and so with an unaltered genetic constitution. Loganberry LY 59, for example, is one genetic individual, one clone, no matter how many thousand separate plants it may be divided into.

COMPOST. Organic matter decomposed to the point where it is immediately available as plant food. Uncomposted material in the soil, fresh straw for instance, will actually *decrease* the supply of plant nutrients for a time until the microbic population has broken it down. ALSO: A prepared growing medium for plants in containers. Purchased composts may be based upon soil, the John Innes (JI) range, or upon peat, as in the soil-less (Levington, Bowers, etc.) types. The latter are lighter and less variable in quality.

DORMANT. Lit. 'sleeping'. Plant in an inactive state owing to low temperature, or a bud which develops when more active growth is pruned away. Plants to be forwarded in warmth—rhubarb, mint, chives, etc.—grow more readily after a period of dormancy.

DRILL. A miniature trench, usually made with a draw-hoe, in which seeds are sown. Wide drills for peas and beans are made with the flat of the hoe blade, narrow drills for small seeds with the corner. Maximum depth for the largest seed should not be more than 2 in. Water the bottom of the drill before sowing in dry weather.

FERTILIZER. Usually applied to inorganic plant food produced chemically from mineral substances or by the fixation of atmospheric nitrogen. Principal elements; nitrogen, phosphorous, potash—NPK—but trace elements now added. Now increasingly accepted that reliance upon fertilizers to the exclusion of organic manures is harmful to soil fertility and structure.

HUMUS. Essential part of all fertile soils. It can be formed only by the breakdown of animal and vegetable matter.

HYBRID. Variety produced by interbreeding of other varieties. F_1 hybrids are the progeny of two distinct and controlled parent lines. Therefore an F_1 hybrid cannot reproduce itself and seed from it should never be saved. Also, F_1 hybrid seed is bound to be expensive because cross-fertilization of the parent strains must be carried out by hand. Many of the best new varieties are of this type of hybrid.

LATERAL. A side-shoot. Where laterals cannot be allowed to develop into full-size branches, as in grape vines and cordon fruit trees, they are regularly pruned back.

LEADER. The growing upper part of a main stem, as opposed to sideways-growing laterals.

LEGUMES or Leguminosae. Pod-bearing plants such as beans. The seeds of legumes are the richest source of vegetable proteins. Their roots bear small lumps or tubercles containing bacteria which extract nitrogen from the air, thereby adding to the food supply both of the plant and of the soil when the roots decay. Legumes require adequate lime in the soil, and enough organic matter to set up the valuable partnership with the bacteria.

pH. Formula used to express the amount of lime in the soil. Above pH 7 the soil is alkaline; below that it is acid and may need liming. Most vegetables prefer a slightly acid pH 6·5, but legumes and the cabbage family need rather more lime. Really acid or 'sour' soils occur frequently in town gardens and must receive not only lime but compost or organic manures to restore them. It is not always realized that a good population of earthworms helps to maintain the alkaline balance of soil through the action of their chalk glands, but there will be no earthworms without humus to feed upon. A simple soil testing kit can be bought for about 25p (see 'Suppliers').

POLLINATION: Fertilization of seed by the transference of pollen from male to female organs. This may take place within one flower, or between separate flowers where they are single-sexed, as in marrows and melons. In many varieties of fruit the flowers, although bi-sexual, cannot pollinate themselves (self-sterile) and require pollen from another variety to make the fruit swell. This pollen must be of a 'compatible' type, and of course the varieties must come into flower at the same time.

SEED-LEAF. The embryo leaf or cotyledon which emerges on germination. It is usually shaped differently to the true leaves and contains the food reserve of the baby plant. Damage to the cotyledons is therefore a severe setback. While in the seed-leaf stage the plant's roots are only just beginning to develop, so this is the best time to transplant seedlings ('pricking out') with a minimum of root damage.

STATION. A point at which seeds are sown, or a position prepared for a plant. Seeds dropped in groups at 1 ft. intervals along a drill to reduce subsequent thinning are at '1 ft. stations'. A soil-covered mound of manure or compost for a cucumber plant is a 'prepared station'.

STOP. To remove the growing point, as from the main stem of a tomato when it has set enough fruit.

SUBSOIL. The relatively infertile layer of soil beginning about a foot down. It may be of clay, chalk, or gravel, and is a source of important minerals to deep-rooted plants. It does not contain the main plant foods, however, and should not be brought to the surface when digging. Clay subsoils are often impervious to water, so that the topsoil is sour and undrained. The subsoil must then be moved and broken up without altering its position.

TILTH. A favourite word in gardening literature but not always obtainable in fact. It means a finely-divided, friable layer of soil just right for the sowing and germination of seeds. A tilth may be 'forced' by mechanical action such as raking, but the resultant soil particles are then often hard and knobbly. A natural tilth is obtained by leaving the soil in lumps after autumn digging. When the clods freeze the water in them expands and shatters them into fine particles. The clods then break down at a touch when the surface has dried in the spring.

CHAPTER TWO

Fruit

FAMILIAR TOP FRUITS

Apples
Pears
Plums
Cherries

LESS FAMILIAR FRUITS

Peaches
Apricots
Figs
Grapes

SOFT FRUITS

Strawberries
Raspberries
Loganberries
Gooseberries and Currants
Rhubarb
Training Fruit Trees on Walls and Fences
Pests and Diseases of Fruit

Fruit

Fresh fruit is perhaps the most valuable and satisfying of garden products and the growing of it an absorbing and enduring interest.

Town gardeners often believe themselves debarred from fruit growing by lack of room, maybe because they think in terms of large orchard trees. In reality, fruit has become an important element in the concept of 'vertical gardening'—the choice of crops which develop upwards from a small base area of precious soil.

A walk down any town or suburban road of high-density building and small gardens reveals much unused fence and wall space, often of good aspect, tatty climbers ready for replacement by something of use and beauty, and dingy evergreens where a bush apple should be scenting the air in spring.

Today's nurserymen cater for the amateur with quick-maturing trees on dwarfing stocks, and a wide selection of cordon and fan-trained varieties, new hardy grape-vines, and trees in pots. They may seem initially expensive, but a three-year-old tree represents an awful lot of work and the buyer should see it for what it is—a 'growth investment'.

Fruit trees in pots are dealt with separately in Chapter 6.

FAMILIAR TOP FRUITS

APPLES

The apple does well on most soils, even quite poor ones provided they are not waterlogged. Luxuriant growth is not wanted and the best dessert fruit are produced under fairly dry conditions.

Sizes, Shapes and Rootstocks. The adult size of an apple tree is determined by the rootstock on which it is grafted. You will want a small tree which will come into bearing quickly and for this you ask for an M.26 or M.7 stock. A bush tree on M.26 will come into bearing eighteen months after planting

37

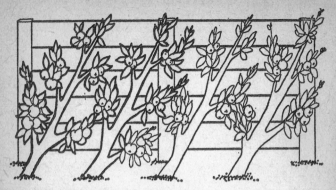

Cordon apples on posts and wire, forming screen

in a good soil: on M.7 the tree will be somewhat larger and slower starting.

The shape of the tree also has a bearing on the amount of space it will occupy. The big standard and half-standard types are only for the orchard and large garden, for us the choice must be between the bush and the cordon. The bush has a very short trunk and spreading, easy-to-get-at branches; you must visualize it filling a circle at least 8 ft. in diameter and you cannot plant it where you hope to grow vegetables. The single stem cordon bears its fruit on short laterals and needs a planting space of only 2 ft. It is not always realized that a 12 ft. stretch—the width of a smallish room—will take seven cordon apple trees. They will fit into a narrow border against a south or west facing wall or fence, or can form a screen if trained up a simple erection of posts and horizontal wires.

Another alternative is the Family Tree. This is a dwarfing stock grafted with three different varieties, in effect three apple trees in one. Laxton and Bunyard (see Suppliers) offer five different combinations of dessert and cooking varieties, selected for ability to pollinate one another, and to give a choice in season of use.

Pollination. Not many apples and pears are completely self-fertile. Pollen has to be transferred to the flowers from other trees and these must be of suitable varieties. Where plenty of apples grow in surrounding gardens this is no problem, but infertility in a single tree is usually the result of bad pollination. With the Family Tree the matter is taken care of, but in planting separate varieties choose those known to cross-pollinate. Some reliable ones are given below.

Variety	Season of use	Pollinator
Laxtons Superb	Dec.–Feb.	Moderately
Usually crops alternate years		self-fertile
Ellisons Orange	Oct.	Moderately
Unusual aniseed flavour		self-fertile
Cox's Orange Pippin	Nov.–Jan.	Worcester
Temperamental		Pearmain
Charles Ross	Oct.–Dec.	Cox's Orange
Very large. Yellowish red		Pippin
Golden Delicious	Nov.–Feb.	Charles Ross
Favourite import		
James Grieve	Sept.–Oct.	Epicure
Best substitute for Cox's		Charles Ross
Egremont Russet	Oct.–Nov.	Lord Lambourne
Fine flavour. Compact tree		
Lord Lambourne	Oct.–Nov.	Egremont Russet
Large. Good flavour		Ellisons Orange
Grenadier	Aug.–Sept.	Charles Ross
Earliest cooking apple		Ellisons Orange
Lanes Prince Albert	Nov.–Feb.	James Grieve
Best keeping cooker		
for small gardens		

Soil and Planting. Special manuring is unnecessary, though in very light sandy soils some compost may be mixed in with the topsoil during planting. This is also advisable if you are planting a tree on M.9 stock which needs generous treatment at the beginning.

Planting takes place between November and March at any time when the ground is not frozen. Dig a hole wide enough to take the roots fully spread out and deep enough for the tree to go in up to the soil mark on the stem. Break up the subsoil at the bottom of the hole. Put the tree in position, and, if a bush tree, drive in a good stake and tie the tree to it before filling in the hole. Special tying materials can be bought, but a nylon stocking is as good as any of them. Give it two turns round the stake, once round the tree, and tie with a reef knot. It is soft, grips firmly, stretches a little, and lasts for years.

Fill in with friable soil, sifting it among the roots and treading it gently as you go. Finish off with a mulch of peat or garden compost. Newly-planted trees must not be allowed to dry out during their first summer; give an occasional good soaking through the mulch and spray or sprinkle the foliage whenever you have time in hot, sunny spells.

Single cordon trees are planted with the stem at an angle of 45 degrees, even if the direction has to be altered later. This has the effect of restricting vegetative growth and encouraging the formation of fruiting spurs.

The same planting rules apply to all fruit trees, with some variation for pot-grown figs and grapes.

Pruning. Over-zealous pruning of bush trees results in more wood and less fruit. Limit it to keeping the main branches from getting over-crowded and crossing one another.

Cordons have to develop clusters of fruiting spurs all the way up their stems and cannot be allowed long lateral branches. The way to achieve this is by summer pruning. When a tree is pruned in winter it is stimulated into growing more vigorously; but if its young shoots are pruned in summer it is checked rather than stimulated and the check causes it to develop more fruit buds. All the side shoots on a cordon should be shortened by cutting back the *new* growth some 4 to 6 leaves in late July. In winter the laterals may be shortened a little more, leaving stubby spurs with fat fruit buds. All pruning cuts should be made just above a bud and you shouldn't prune during hard frost.

Harvesting. Pick apples only when fully ripe, the full flavour which is a reason for growing your own will then have had time to develop. The test of ripeness is to lift the apple up gently until its stalk is horizontal; if it then comes away from the tree without tugging it's ripe.

PEARS

This lovely fruit is neglected. A perfectly ripened pear, in the condition in which, as Mr. Fred Streeter has said, the juice runs down to your feet when you bite it, is something to be proud of.

In 1885 the R.H.S. held a national pear conference. The number of different varieties exhibited was 616; nowadays we should be hard put to it to name six, and one of those would be Conference, so called after that particular exhibition.

Pears grown as bush trees are over-large for our purpose but the cordon form is ideal if you can find wall space for it, or preferably for two of different varieties to ensure pollination. The warmth and shelter of a wall has always been recognized as a factor in growing good pears.

General Cultivation. No special soil requirements, but make sure that there is free drainage under the roots. An annual dose of any organic manure lightly forked in will pay higher dividends with pears than with apples.

Planting is the same as for apples. Try to arrange for the young tree to start off in an oblique direction by planting it about 2 ft. to one side of the vertical line up which it is eventually to grow. Tie it to bamboo stakes for the first two years if wall fastenings are difficult. Plant with the stem at least 4 in. from the wall.

Cordon Pear in space between two windows showing how young tree was planted in oblique position

Varieties and Pollination. Williams Bon Chrétien, despite its French name, is one good thing to have come from the village of Aldermaston. It arrived about 1770 and is still a favourite for Sept.–Oct. use. Others are Conference, Oct.–Dec.; Doyenné du Comice, Nov.–Dec.; Bristol Cross and Packhams Triumph, Nov.

Conference and Williams are both partially self-fertile, and effectively pollinate one another. If I had to settle for a single tree it would be Conference. Bristol Cross is a new variety and a very good cropper, but it will not pollinate others. Comice is supposed to be the epicure's pear, but it really only succeeds in the south of the country and even there is an irregular bearer. This is mainly due to the short time for which its flowers are receptive of fertilization, only a single day compared with seven days for Packhams Triumph and nine for Bristol Cross. Packhams is an Australian introduction, quite at home here and a regular cropper. In quality it approaches Comice and its fine clusters of blossom make it one of the most decorative fruit trees in spring.

Probably the largest pear in cultivation is Pitmaston Duchess. It's excellent eating and a reliable variety, though perhaps less consistent than Conference, Williams, and Packhams, the trio from which I would always choose.

Pruning and Harvesting. Pruning of cordon pears is the same as for apples, the side growths being shortened in summer and cut back further if neccessary in winter. I would advise against planting double cordons; the initial management of two stems is more awkward and if you have the space available it's more profitable to go for two single cordons of different varieties.

Pick pears when they come away easily with a slight twist, being very careful not to bruise them. Store in the coolest room of the house and—*watch them*. Test for ripeness by pressing gently at the stalk end and when one ripe one has been found examine them every day.

PLUMS

They like an alkaline soil, so if you have to garden on chalk are a sensible choice. Another reason for growing dessert plums is the apparent impossibility of buying any worth eating. At a time of year when shops are crammed with imported peaches any enquiry for plums is regarded as the height of eccentricity, yet what could be better than a sun-warmed ripe Victoria eaten straight from the tree?

Varieties and Pollination. Fortunately, two of the best dessert plums, Victoria and Oullins Golden Gage, are both self-fertile and can be grown on their own. Victoria is the most reliable; she has her illustrious namesake's sense of duty and is the unquestioned choice if you are limited to a single tree. The two mentioned form a succession, Oullins ripening in August and Victoria in September. There is one later dessert plum, Coe's Golden Drop, which may sometimes be picked in early October. It has a yellow skin spotted with red, rather a tough skin, too, but its contents are the sweetest and juiciest of any British plum. It is not self-fertile and must have other varieties nearby to set fruit.

Cooking plums *can* be bought and are out of place in the small garden.

Soil and Cultivation. If you are on a peaty or very sandy soil a dressing of 4 oz. of hydrated lime per sq. yd. should be forked into the planting site and repeated at least every other year. Plums under these conditions may also suffer nitrogen and potash deficiencies and a couple of good handfuls of a high-potash fish manure should be forked in around the tree in spring. On heavier soils, especially those with a chalk subsoil plums look after themselves very well. This spring dose of fish manure, however, probably pays off with most fruits. They are admittedly better without too much nitrogen, which encourages leafy growth, but adequate potash supplies are essential.

Try to get plums planted in the autumn, remembering that they start into growth very early and that this is a strain when roots have not had time to settle.

Shapes and Pruning. Bush plum trees don't take up too much room and a fan-trained Victoria is also an excellent wall tree. Plums, like the other main stone fruits, peaches and cherries, are not grown as cordons.

Pruning of all stone fruit should be kept to the minimum needed to maintain the shape of the tree and to remove broken, diseased, or overcrowded branches. *All* pruning of plums and cherries should be done in the summer to minimize the risk of Silver Leaf. This is a fungus disease which enters by unhealed wounds, so any cuts should be made at a time of year when a protective cell layer will quickly grow over them. The exposed surfaces should be immediately covered with paint.

43

There is no dwarfing stock for cherries and commercially they are all grown on large orchard trees. As wall trees they can be kept within bounds, and many nurserymen offer fan trained specimens for this purpose.

The dark red, acid flavoured Morello is always suggested as the suitable occupant for a north wall, and is indeed quite happy there. Its fruit is not particularly useful, even if it is the right species for making cherry jam, and one reason for its frequent presence in Victorian walled gardens is now overlooked. The Morello is not only the one self-fertile cherry, it also pollinates sweet cherries blooming at the same time. Growing on a north wall it could pollinate fine dessert varieties on the south and west walls.

The wall culture of fine dessert cherries is now rather unusual but is similar to that of plums in regard to soil and cultivation. Except for the self-fertile Morello the trouble is pollination.

The breeding habits of cherries are so complex that only the nurseryman can properly advise you. Briefly, you can grow a Morello on its own, or a dessert variety and a Morello, or two sweet varieties if they belong to different groups. Varieties in the same group won't cross-fertilize. Catalogues usually explain which to grow with which.

LESS FAMILIAR FRUITS

PEACHES

In the southern half of England peaches fruit satisfactorily as bush trees in open sunny positions. The shelter of a wall may give even better results, and in some seasons the town peach succeeds where its country cousin fails. Spring frosts are a major danger to its very early blossom and, in the larger urban areas at least, town night temperatures are those few vital degrees higher.

Type of Tree. If a south or west wall is available the fan-trained tree will ripen its fruit in all but the worst summers. A bush tree needs a position in which it gets all the sun there is, especially in late summer. Both peaches and nectarines are self-fertile.

Soil and Planting. Exactly the same soil requirements as plums, except that the peach is greedier. An annual mulch of compost, plus the spring dose of fish manure, should be given. The peach fruits on young wood grown the previous season. This means encouraging it to make more growth than you want from other top fruits. Well-fed peach trees are also healthier than half-starved ones.

Peaches don't like being moved, and a number of young trees must be lost yearly through slapdash planting. Arrange for delivery early in the autumn and plant as soon as the tree or trees arrive. Trim off any damaged roots and have a pailful of fine soil and garden compost for use during the filling-in. If the soil of the planting site is sticky or lumpy the purchase of 28 lb. of JI potting compost might be justified for this purpose; as a young fan-trained peach will cost upwards of £2·50 it will be no extravagance to give it a good start.

The topmost roots should be 4 in. below the surface after planting. Firm the soil by gently treading, make sure that it is thoroughly moist, and spread a 2 in. peat mulch around the tree to protect the roots further from very hard frost. Stake and tie a bush tree no matter how small it may look.

In the spring any blossoms should be picked off (though they will probably drop anyway) and the soil under the peat kept consistently moist.

The cheapest form of tree to buy and the easiest to transplant is the maiden. This will have a length of stem and a few little twigs near the top, the product of one year's growth since grafting. It will make a bush tree with time and very little trouble, but it takes three years of careful pruning to lay down the basic shape of a wall tree.

Peach trees grow easily from stones, but it's only an outside chance that the resultant tree will be worth the six years' waiting before it fruits. You will shorten the odds against success by planting the stones of English peaches only.

Pruning. Bush trees need only the cutting out of dead wood and the prompt removal of shoots whose leaves or leaf buds appear to be dying. This is the condition known as Die-back and the affected twigs should be cut hard back. If any part of the tree appears to be getting overcrowded some of the current year's growth maybe thinned out in late summer, remembering that you have to leave enough of it for next year's crop.

45

In established wall trees which have filled their allotted space you have to encourage new (fruiting-next-year) wood and train it in to replace the old (fruited-this-year) wood. From near the base of each fruiting shoot allow one good new shoot to grow. Stop any others by nipping out their tips in summer. After the leaves have fallen the old fruiting branch is cut right out and the new growth, the 'replacement shoot', is trained in its place. Without regular pruning wall peaches tend to become a tangle of old and new growth with ever fewer ripe fruit.

Varieties. For northern or cold districts, the early ripening Alexander, or Hales Early. Elsewhere, Peregrine or the yellow fleshed Bellegarde. Hales Early and Peregrine are the two most widely grown outdoors.

Nectarines are a slightly different form of peach. Their skin is smooth, not downy, and some people prefer their flavour to that of the peach. The only difference in cultivation is that nectarines should be kept well watered while the fruit is swelling or it may split. Peaches tolerate fairly dry conditions at that time. Reliable varieties are Early Rivers, and Humboldt for a late one.

APRICOTS

Apricots are grown only on walls, but this is more to ripen the fruit than to protect the tree. It will in fact grow in the open in most parts of the British Isles, having been brought here from Asia in the reign of Henry VIII. N. B. Bagenal, in his standard work *Fruit Growing*, calls it 'one of the most delicious stone fruits that can be grown in the open'.

Soil and Cultivation. The apricot will thrive wherever plums do well. It requires the same soil and treatment, though it cannot be grown as a bush tree. On poor dry sands it may fail, but the heavy or chalky soils which suit it can be found all over the country. On heavy clay soils which tend to be sour use lime as advised for plums.

Good drainage is essential; when planting in clay take out a foot of subsoil and replace with a mixture of soil, broken brick, mortar rubble and the like. Dust about 8 oz. of bonemeal around the roots while filling in and mulch with peat or garden compost as for peaches.

Pruning. The apricot is more easily managed than the peach.

It forms fruiting spurs on old wood, which of course increases year by year. The tree is allowed to grow until its allotted space on the wall is filled, and pruning is then restricted to training in an occasional new shoot as replacement for a very old or diseased branch and cutting out the young growth which is obviously not wanted. All pruning should be done in the summer.

Varieties. Hemskirk and Moorpark are old favourites, hardy and bearing large orange-red fruit. Two new American varieties being recommended are Alfred and Farmingdale. All apricots are self-fertile.

FIGS

They do well in the South-west and along the South Coast. Even growing on a wall they may need a protective covering in winter. And they *must* be half starved.

The last proviso is important if you have a nice expanse of south-facing wall but no decent soil adjacent to it. Perhaps there's a paved area concealing an accumulation of builders' rubble, but you would still like to see something green against the wall. The place is made for a fig tree.

Soil and Situation. The aim must be to produce branches that are hard and ripened, not soft and sappy. Sun and warmth and hard living are essential. The wild fig will grow on a sheer rock face, and in southern France cultivated varieties flourish in a few inches of dust over rock outcrops.

If your soil is indeed poor and full of brickbats you have only to hack out a big enough hole and dump the tree in it. It will almost certainly be pot-grown, with the roots in a compact ball. Don't spread them out, just fill in around them with a little decent soil or compost and make firm.

In ordinary good garden soil the problem is to restrict the root run. The usual advice is to take out a larger hole than ultimately needed, line the sides with bricks or concrete blocks and the bottom with rubble, and plant in this sort of box. For those who dislike hard work I suggest the following method:

Ask for your tree to be delivered in its pot (normally it would be knocked out to reduce weight in transit). Dig the hole big enough round to take the pot, and about 6 in. deeper. Put a 3 in. layer of gravel or rubble at the bottom and stand

47

the pot on it. Fill in, leaving the rim 3 in. below the surface. The roots will gradually escape from the top into the surrounding soil and if the tree starts growing too exuberantly you have only to scrape a little earth away and cut through some of them where they come over the pot rim.

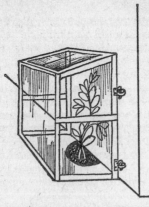

Winter cover for figs or other tender wall fruit. Made of 2 by 2 in. and 2 by 1 in. sawn timber covered with Claritex or reinforced polythene

Autumn is usually recommended for planting, but for a pot-grown tree there is a lot to be said for April. It establishes quickly and you avoid immediate worries about winter protection.

Newly-planted figs need regular watering in dry weather, especially those planted in the pot.

Protection. If growth is cut by frost the coming season's crop will be lost. Traditional protection methods include wrapping the branches in sacking and hanging covers over the tree. Gardeners in northern France used to grow their figs as spreading bushes close to the ground. In winter they were bent down into a shallow trench and all the branches buried. For the town garden the neatest solution is a wooden frame shaped rather like a fireguard, covered with Claritex or a similar plastic. This is made to cover the tree in entirely, held to the wall top and bottom by hooks and eyes. In effect, a very light, narrow, lean-to mini-greenhouse. Put in position about the beginning of December it can be left there until late March. In a built-up area, and with some probable heat loss through the wall, it would limit frost damage in all but the worst cold spells. During these an extra covering can be draped over the tree, safe from being blown off by wind or soaked by melting snow.

Polythene film is not suitable for 'glazing' the frame, it wears badly at points of contact with the woodwork. Wire-reinforced polythene is all right, so is clear semi-rigid P.V.C. I have seen a fig tree adequately protected by a frame covered with Windolite, though this material is now less used.

The portable frame can be used to protect early peach and apricot blossom, but should not be placed in position until the flowers are ready to open. Peach and apricot trees soon get too big to permit the use of a frame of manageable size.

Varieties. Brunswick or Brown Turkey. There are others but the beginner would be wise not to attempt them.

GRAPES

The growing of grapes in the open for dessert and wine making has been taken up with enthusiasm in recent years. The enthusiasts take credit for doing what most gardeners believed impossible—the successful culture of the vine in the English climate. In fact, the vine has always been grown in England since Roman times, and in small gardens at that. Writing about 1900, E. T. Cook has this to say:

'East Anglia is one of the parts of England that has always been noted for its open-air Vines, and cottagers sometimes make good sums of money by the sale of grapes from their walls. The Vines generally cover the roof, as well as the front of the cottage, being supported by a wooden framework, about fifteen inches from the roof. Vines delight in abundance of sunshine and should be planted against a wall facing south. A border must be prepared, but this is quite easy as it need not be more than two and a half feet deep and three feet in width. A border of these dimensions, if composed of good holding, heavy soil, with a little bone meal and a liberal quantity of old mortar rubble added, will support Vines for many years, provided the roots are well mulched with short manure. . . . Rich borders encourage a strong sappy growth which does not ripen properly and invariably gets crippled in winter'.

This quotation not only proves the continuity of open-air viticulture, it shows how well the essentials have always been known—exposure to sun, a soil poor rather than too rich, conditions to ripen the canes as well as the fruit. The cultural hints might have come from a contemporary source, except that nowadays we haven't the energy to prepare planting sites 2 ft. 6 in. deep.

Soil and Planting. Good drainage is important and a clay subsoil should be broken up. A pailful of peat and coarse sand can be dug in instead of the traditional 'mortar rubble'.

Buy two-year-old pot-grown vines if possible and plant from October to February. If you receive them with the soil ball intact break it up carefully and spread the roots out, if this is not done moisture may fail to penetrate the ball and the roots will die.

Mulch round the vine with peat or compost and keep this mulch going permanently. If preferred you may cover the ground almost up to the stem with bricks, stone, or concrete slabs. This suits the vine just as well since it needs the mulch more as protection for its shallow roots than as a source of nourishment. These roots are very far-ranging, as anyone who has ever dug up an old greenhouse vine can testify, but they run close to the surface so there must be no deep digging near a vine. Once established, it will find its own living and need neither feeding nor watering.

Situation and Training. A south or west wall is the right position if you live in the Midlands or further north. In southern districts too it increases the range of varieties and the chances of a good crop, but here the vines may also be grown in the open ground and trained on wires or trellis.

For wall training the newly-planted vine is cut back to three buds immediately; this should not be left till spring or the vine may bleed. The buds left will provide shoots to be trained up the wall as cordons in the first summer and provide the permanent framework. Not more than three cordons are grown from each vine, but vines may be planted 4 ft. apart and at this distance will completely cover the chosen area.

The management of the cordon vine is rather similar to that of the apple or pear. The stems will take a year or two to reach a reasonable height and they are then stopped. By now they will be quite thick and woody and from the second season onwards should be fruiting. The young side shoots are stopped in July, those carrying fruit being cut back to a few leaves beyond the *first* fruit bunch. Superfluous side shoots may be trimmed back at any time in the summer. Winter pruning consists of cutting back every side growth to two or three buds; this should not be done in severe frost or left until the sap is rising in spring. Given the chance, vines are apt to start bustin' out all over; what is wanted are stout main stems and short laterals restricted to single bunches of fruit.

Wall grapes are most easily trained up trellis fixed well clear of the wall. This makes it easy to support fruiting laterals and looks more appropriate than wires.

The same three-stem cordon system may be used for vines in the open garden, possibly up trellis, arch or pergola, but in an exposed position Dwarf Guyot training may be preferable. In this the two strongest stems are spread out horizontally on either side and tied to wires while the third and weakest stem is cut back to three buds. This is done in the autumn; the following summer the strong stems will fruit and the cut-back one will produce three more stems for the whole process to be repeated in the autumn.

Grapes may be grown under cloches, but the ordinary growers barn cloche is too small and low. Anyone intending to try this method should first study it and then design his own cloches.

Ornamental vines are popular because of their magnificent leaf colours in autumn. Some fruiting varieties can be allowed to grow more or less unhindered in the expectation of ripening a few bunches of grapes without the work of training.

Varieties. Black Hamburgh and Esperione are hardy black grapes. Buckland Sweetwater is a vigorous, large berried white, and Perle de Czaba and Royal Muscadine are hardy, early ripening whites with smaller berries. A newer variety for wine making is Seyve-Villard 5/276, and among the newer outdoor dessert grapes is The Cambridge (Laxton and Bunyard), an October ripening white very suitable for wall growing.

For free-growing ornamental purposes the best choices are Brandt, which some nurserymen list among the ornamental climbers as Vitis Brandt, and Baco No. 1. Brandt has richly coloured autumn foliage and small sweet black berries; Baco is vigorous enough to cover a shed or garage and is also a small black grape. Too acid for dessert, it can produce a useful harvest for the wine-maker.

Pests. Birds and wasps are real menaces. Small mesh netting will defeat the birds, but the enclosure of each ripening bunch in a ventilated polythene fruit bag as recommended for choice pears is the only protection against both. Damage can occur very quickly—I have known wasps to reduce bunches of grapes in a greenhouse to mere clusters of skins in one day.

Newcomers to the growing of this fascinating fruit, so well adapted to the very small garden, should consult The Viticultural Research Station (see Suppliers) for information on varieties, publications and supplies.

SOFT FRUIT

STRAWBERRIES

The queen of the berries, the strawberry should be gathered fully ripe and eaten within an hour or so of picking. Better still, eaten immediately, sun-warm and scented. That is adequate reason for growing your own.

Other reasons are the adaptability of strawberries to unusual methods of growing (see Chapter 6), the fact that no other fruit will crop within months of planting, and the increased length of the strawberry season since the introduction of perpetual or everbearing varieties. It may be said that deep-freeze strawberries are available all the year round, so why bother? Mr. Edward Hyams, in his book *Strawberry Growing Complete* (which you should read if you want fresh strawberries for nine months of the year) says of the deep-frozen ones that to anyone who still has a palate they are worthless. He errs on the side of charity; they are filthy.

Soil and Situation. The wild strawberry is a woodland plant, growing in leaf mould. Its descendants also need a soil full of humus, rather acid, and a good sponge for moisture.

Whatever your own soil, you can grow strawberries if you dig in enough compost, peat, rotted manure, hop manure, or other bulky organic material. On thin chalky soils you need a lot more, on heavy loams or naturally peaty soils somewhat less. A small barrowload of compost per square yard would be a fair average. Before planting, fork in 2 oz. of fish manure and 2 oz. of fine bone meal per sq. yd. Mulch with sedge peat all round the plants every spring, it keeps the berries cleaner and builds up the necessary humus.

Sun is vital for the ripening and flavour of strawberries, but this does not mean that they must have uninterrupted sun all day. I have picked very good berries on a site which got no sun at all for many hours in the middle of the day.

Planting and Cultivation. There are three main types of strawberry; the June-fruiters, which provide early strawberries under glass and also the ordinary summer crop; the perpetuals, which begin fruiting in late summer and continue through the autumn; and the alpines, which have small berries intermittently through the summer, are decorative little plants useful for edging flower beds.

The June-fruiters are planted in August or September, the earlier the better. Order in good time from a nurseryman supplying Certified or S.S. (virus-free) plants. They will be runners rooted that summer and you want to get them well established before winter. Have the site prepared, plant with the trowel at a depth which completely covers the roots but does not bury the little plant's central bud. Water well after planting and every few days thereafter in dry weather, this is very important with an August planting.

Spacing depends on the layout adopted. You can have the individual row, with each plant standing separate and its runners removed as they grow. Or the matted row, in which runners are allowed to take root and form a mat of plants of differing ages. From a limited area of ground this method gives the greatest return.

For a matted row in the open, i.e. not to be cloched, two rows are planted 18 in. apart. The plants in them are 1 ft. apart in staggered formation. If planted before the end of September these maidens will crop the following June. About that time they will begin to make stolons or runners which become new plants. Visualize a strip about 3 ft. wide and keep the runners within that limit. By the end of the summer you will have a mat of old and young plants, all of which will fruit the following year.

For cloching you plant one row 9 in. apart and allow it to develop a mat 2 ft. wide, by the second year. Cloche in March and keep well watered. Mulch with peat to conserve moisture

53

and provide a clean surface for those berries which touch the ground. Space the cloches $\frac{1}{2}$ in. apart in hot weather and shade by painting them lightly with limewash; strawberries under glass are literally cooked in hot sun.

The oldest plants in a matted row can be dug out after the second year, and any perennial weeds should also be removed. Any gaps are soon closed.

Perpetuals. Late summer and autumn fruiting. The berries are as large as those of the June-fruiters, the plants vigorous and crops in a good season enormous.

Plant in autumn if possible, at least 18 in. apart in the row. It is also possible to plant in spring and pick fruit the same year. Perpetuals are weakly looking things in April, but by May they start to grow and blossom. *Pick off all these flowers as they come until early August.* By then the plants will have grown and made runners; parents and runners alike will flower and set fruit, sometimes for the next two or three months. The yield can be very large, but soil must be good and the plants never allowed to get dry. The perpetual strawberry is a fascinating fruit. I have picked in the open in November, and dug up fruiting plants to finish in the greenhouse in December.

Because of its speed of growth the perpetual is best propagated annually by planting runners in the autumn and scrapping the old plants.

Alpines. These may be bought as plants or raised from seed (see Chapter 5). They do not make runners. The berries are small and produced at intervals throughout the summer. In terms of quantity they are hardly worth growing, but many people value them and the *fraises des bois*, which are really the same thing, are still flown in from the Continent. Alpines are pretty little plants with dainty flower clusters set off by pale green foliage. Once established they usually seed themselves and pop up in unexpected places.

Protection from Birds and Slugs. Strawberries must be netted against birds when not cloched. The best arrangement is a frame about 18 in. high made of light battens and covered with nylon netting which can be removed after fruiting and will last for years. It's no use simply throwing the netting over the strawberry bed so that it rests on the plants. The birds will sit on it and peck the berries and you will pull some of the fruit off when you lift it. Put out food and water for birds when you have soft fruit ripening. Thirst and the feeding of voracious young make them determined robbers. (I have seen a blackbird trying to ram a whole strawberry down the throat of an offspring as large as itself.)

Slug bait should be put down when berries start to ripen. The use of straw to protect from slugs and dirt is impracticable in the matted row and untidy in the small garden. Wire supports for the fruit can be bought but are expensive; a few yards of stiff galvanized wire snipped into 8 in. lengths makes dozens of the simple gadget. This is quickly put under the developing fruit and keeps the truss safe from slugs and in a cleaner and drier condition than on straw.

Varieties. June-fruiters: the one most grown commercially is Cambridge Favourite. It is criticized by those who have not eaten it really fresh and perfectly ripened but I have grown it since the days when it was known only by a number and still think it has every good quality. Cambridge Vigour is slightly earlier and good for cloches, it can also be planted as late as October with the hope of a crop the following year. Royal Sovereign is still grown but doesn't crop like the Cambridge varieties. Talisman is reliable and slightly later.

Perpetuals (also known as remontants or everbearers): Sans Rivale and St. Claude were two early French introductions; the first is very strong and prolific, distinctively flavoured with strongly scented fruit and blossom. One of the best English-bred varieties is Hampshire Maid.

The only alpine usually offered is Baron Solemacher. It is said to make wonderful jam—if you can collect enough of it—because of its unusually high pectin content. A new variety you can raise from seed is Delicious (Dobies).

RASPBERRIES

One of the very few fruits whose flavour survives canning or freezing substantially unaltered and so has a low priority in the very small garden. I include it as a suggestion for those who have to cope with cool, damp summers, or who want to make use of a predominantly shady patch. These are the sort of conditions the raspberry will put up with.

Soil and Cultivation. Same soil as strawberries—plenty of humus-forming material dug in before planting. Equally important is a compost or peat mulch extending at least a foot along both sides of a raspberry row. They are about the shallowest-rooting of all fruits, with a mat of feeding roots just below the surface. If this vulnerable root layer is allowed to become dry and starved the crop will fail. Put down a 2 in. thick surround of organic material in the spring and supply plenty of water when the fruit is swelling.

Because of the shallow roots there must be no deep cultivation near the canes. Weeds should be hoed up or hand-pulled, the mulch making this much easier for even perennial weeds like docks can be pulled from ground consistently mulched.

Planting and Subsequent Work. Plant the canes in autumn 18 in. apart. You are unlikely to have room for more than one row, but if this is your intention remember that the rows must be 4 ft. apart. A dressing of 2 oz. per yard run of fish manure or hoof and horn, forked in before planting, will encourage cane growth. Plant with the top roots only 1 in. below the surface, treading them in firmly and firming them again if frost loosens them during the winter. Cut the canes down to 1 ft. from the ground after planting. This means no fruit in the first year when the object is to build up strong canes.

Old canes are cut out every year after fruiting and the sooner this is done the better chance have the young canes to grow and ripen their wood in readiness for a good crop the following year. The canes have to be supported, either by being tied to wires or by being trained up through two sets of parallel wires, which obviates the chore of tying.

Raspberries need protection from birds with small mesh netting and should be picked every two or three days once they start to ripen.

Varieties. Malling Promise and Norfolk Giant are both heavy croppers, Norfolk Giant being the later by about ten days. There is an interesting and very good flavoured yellow variety called Golden Everest. Autumn fruiting types have long been grown and the newest one is Zeva. Amateur growers have reported enthusiastically on its large, dark red berries, borne from September until the frosts come in November.

LOGANBERRIES

The loganberry and the cultivated blackberry are treated in exactly the same way but the loganberry is slightly the more manageable in a limited space and from the culinary point of view the more worth growing. It does well on any boundary fence except one facing due north, and its large dark red berries have a rich, distinctive, sub-acid flavour when cooked. Trained on posts and wires it makes a quick-growing screen.

It was introduced in 1897. Some accounts say that Judge Logan of California bred it by crossing a raspberry with a blackberry, others that he just happened on it growing wild. It was widely planted in small gardens up to thirty years ago —I recollect fine examples in town gardens in Acton and Brentford—but it contracted a virus disease which so reduced its cropping powers that it became hardly worth growing. In the 1950s a virus-free clone was marketed and it is now due for a comeback.

Soil and Cultivation. Exactly as for the raspberry. The logan may be larger, tougher and deeper-rooting, but it needs the same humus-rich soil, the same moisture and the same summer mulch. The last should be easy because you will have room for only one or two plants.

Plant in autumn and cut down to a foot as for raspberries. Planting may be delayed until February if weather is very bad. Give water when needed during the first summer and tie the long prickly canes to their supports as they grow; at that stage they are soft and easily damaged.

Training. This must be systematic or the logan will look untidy and picking become hazardous. The old canes are cut out at ground level as soon as they finish fruiting, some time in August. Before this, however, the new canes are lengthening and must be stowed out of the way and out of danger. On a fence or trellis 5 or 6 ft. high they should be trained at different levels. One year's canes are spread out on either side up to a height of about 3 ft. and the new growth of the following year is led through them and spread out in the vacant space above this height. Next year the positions are reversed.

Varieties. The only certified virus-free loganberry is L.Y. 59 and most nurserymen now stock it. Don't be put off with anything else. There is a thornless loganberry; I have planted it and would not do so again, though a good thornless type will no doubt appear one day.

Among blackberries, Himalayan Giant is the heaviest cropper but is an unwieldy brute to manage. I would choose between Bedford Giant and John Innes, the first early and the second very late.

Blackcurrants are unfortunately 'out' for the smallest gardens. They can only be grown as large, spreading bushes which must be planted at least 5 ft. apart and so don't give an adequate return on the space they occupy.

Gooseberries and red and white currants are different; they can be trained and pruned into cordon and standard forms that take up only a fraction of the space needed to grow them as bushes.

Gooseberries. Green gooseberries are not worth growing, they can be bought cheaply and, thanks to their hardness, in better condition than any other 'soft' fruit. Good dessert gooseberries, however, are becoming rare in the shops, and it is hard to believe that amateur societies devoted entirely to gooseberry-culture once existed.

Soil for gooseberries must be well-drained and rich in potash. Garden compost and wood ashes dug in well before planting in the autumn are the best preparatory dressings. Follow up with top dressings of high-potash fish manure every spring—a handful forked in around each. Too much nitrogen without potash produces lots of growth at the expense of fruit.

Cordons can be bought from most major nurserymen. The single cordons are planted only 15 in. apart against a wall or fence and the triple (three-stemmed) form about 3 ft. apart. Standards are like small standard rose trees and may be planted 3 ft. apart and interplanted with low-growing annual flowers.

Pruning of cordons is similar to that of cordon top fruit. All side-shoots are pinched back to within 5 in. of the main stem in June or July, and cut back to within 2 in. of it during the winter. Fruit is borne on both year-old and older wood, and the aim of pruning is to get an even crop of berries all the way up the stem. Not too many, because you want large, perfectly ripened ones. The leader at the top of the stem is shortened by about half the new growth made each year. The branches of the standard are pruned individually in the same way as the cordon. All sucker growth coming up from the ground is cut away immediately. One advantage of growing gooseberries on these trained trees is that you don't have to tear your hands to pieces when picking.

Red and White Currants. The white is really a variety of the red, and there is little difference in flavour. Both reds and whites can be obtained as cordons, and cultivation is the same as for gooseberries. Currants suffer more from drought, and a summer mulch of compost is always welcome. They do well against a north wall, coming a little later than on a south or west one. For single cordons, planting may be as close as 1 ft.

Varieties. Gooseberries: Leveller, with Lancashire Lad as second choice. Red currants: Laxtons No. 1. White: White Versailles.

RHUBARB

Botanists may go berserk at the inclusion of an edible leaf stalk among the fruits, but if a thing is cooked as a fruit and eaten as a fruit, then to me it's a fruit.

Early rhubarb is truly a first-fruit, and as such very welcome. Its appearance in spring is a promise of things to come.

Soil and Cultivation. It will survive under most conditions but only gives of its best in a well-fed soil with a free run for its big fleshy roots. Prepare the ground by digging in compost and using a nitrogenous organic like dried blood or hoof and horn before planting. Remove all perennial weeds and break up the subsoil. Situation is not important, but a completely shady site is bad. Watering is usually unnecessary once the roots have got well down. The large leaves are designed to catch the rain and transport it back to the crowns. A dressing of rotted manure or compost should be given annually in autumn.

Planting. Plant in autumn, with the crowns 2 ft. apart. If you have a friend who grows it, persuade him to dig up one or two older crowns, divide and replant and give you the surplus pieces. If you buy from a nursery, insist on 'crowns' or 'stools' rather than 'sets'. The crown is a mass of root and buds which will be in full production eighteen months after planting; the set is a single bud with a few inches of trimmed root which may be two to three years reaching full production.

No sticks should be pulled in the first year after planting, the growth is all needed to build up a strong base for years of future cropping. Once established the only attention needed is weeding and the yearly compost.

Forwarding and Forcing. Rhubarb is forwarded by covering the crowns in early spring with straw, which I don't recommend, or with something big enough for the sticks to attain a good length in complete darkness. Wooden boxes or barrels, 5 gallon oil drums with one end cut out and the insides cleaned by burning, old dustbins even. Place the covers in position in mid-February and pulling should start in a month. Remove the covers in late April. One is told that if this is done annually the rhubarb deteriorates; I can only say that my own roots have been forwarded every year for a long time and are as vigorous as ever.

Forcing is done by digging up the entire root and bringing it indoors (see Chapter 5). A root which has been forced will eventually recover if replanted, but it is better to force the oldest and biggest crowns and to divide one crown each year to have replacements coming along.

Early rhubarb is more attractive-looking and needs less sweetening than the later pullings.

Varieties. Choose from Royal Albert, Champagne, and Timperley Early. The last is a relative newcomer and the earliest yet. The variety Glaskin's Perpetual is easily grown from seed. It is precocious and I have had it produce usable sticks within two years of sowing, but it is not a particularly strong grower. Seed of Holstein Bloodred, a more robust type, is now available from Dobies of Chester. (A 5p packet should give you about forty plants!)

TRAINING FRUIT TREES ON WALLS AND FENCES

Fruit trees are no more harmful to the walls of the dwelling-house than, say, climbing roses or pyracantha. They do, however, need properly securing if the branches are to be kept evenly spaced and are not to be dragged away from the wall by the weight of fruit.

Various patent ties exist, but fillis string, tarred or otherwise, attached to wall nails, is adaptable to all sizes and situations. The type of nail to use is either the 'vine eye' which has an eye for threading the string through, or the lead-headed wall nail. The latter is smaller and cheaper and quite adequate. Nor will it damage either brickwork or rendered walls. Both types may be bought from Woodmans if your local shops don't stock them.

If a special bed is made up against a house wall for tree-planting be careful not to raise its level above that of the damp course.

Training on a boundary fence which has to be painted or treated with preservative is a problem. Panels of Weldmesh or Gro-Mesh fixed just clear of the fence on wooden blocks are a neat solution. If the entire panel, with its attached canes or branches, is made detachable from the fence, the whole set-up can be bent gently forward without damage and the fence repainted. Cuprinol is a safer preservative here than creosote or any coal-tar derivative.

PESTS AND DISEASES OF FRUIT

Apples. The textbooks tell us of at least twenty plagues and recommend an arsenal of chemicals. Commercial growers have increasing trouble with resistant strains of pests, and meanwhile we are advised not to eat the skins of bought apples—which contain much of the vitamin C—for fear of poisonous residues.

Spraying with tar-oil winter wash destroys some pests and eggs and generally cleans up the tree while leaving no persistent poisons. It is not an adequate control of the codling moth and the possibility of the occasional maggot must be faced if you don't want an elaborate spraying programme in the spring and summer.

Apple scab, which browns and cracks the skin, is a fungus disease calling for still more sprays. However, it varies in effects with the season's weather and the susceptibility of the variety. Cox's is one of the worst, and Laxton's Epicure and Charles Ross are among the most resistant. Nor have I ever seen really bad scab on that fine early apple James Grieve. A mild case of scab doesn't spoil the crop, but it may open the way for other diseases in the tree. Resistant varieties, a dry, sunny position, no over-feeding, and pruning that keeps branches well spaced so that the foliage dries out after rain are the best preventatives.

Pears. No serious diseases. Choice dessert fruit are often attacked by birds and may have to be protected by netting or by enclosing individual fruits in the ventilated polythene bags sold for the purpose.

Plums. As we have already noted, the infective spores of silver leaf gain admittance through unhealed cuts. The disease is easy to spot, the leaves take on a whitish mildewed look and an entire branch may die. Cut it off during the summer, beyond the affected part, and paint the wound. Victoria is very subject to silver leaf but prompt cutting out can prevent it spreading. All infected wood should be burnt immediately.

Aphis are sometimes a nuisance on plums, blackening the leaves with a sticky substance called 'honeydew'. Spray with 5 per cent tar-oil emulsion in January.

Peaches. The commonest trouble is leaf curl. This sometimes attacks young, newly-planted trees and may then cause a severe check. Affected leaves are curled, thickened, reddened and eventually drop. Spray with lime sulphur or Bordeaux mixture in March and October and collect and burn fallen leaves. The adult tree tends to grow out of the trouble after a year or two's treatment.

Die-back is less common but potentially more dangerous than leaf curl. The symptoms appear in late spring when shoots fail to develop healthy leaves and eventually shrivel and die. Sharp observation and prompt cutting back of affected shoots several inches into healthy wood are the real cures. A well-fed tree will shrug off the condition; keep well mulched with compost and fork in an annual spring dressing of high potash fish manure.

Strawberries. The greatest losses of fruit are due to slugs and birds, which we have already thought about. Next comes botrytis or grey mould, a destructive wet-weather fungus which rots the berries. It can be even worse under cloches than in the open if the season is sunless and condensation hangs all day on fruit and foliage. Ventilate by spacing the cloches and remove a few leaves if the foliage is so dense that the berries are getting no light. In the open, use wire supports so that sun can reach the berries and air circulate around them. Pick off any berries showing brown patches at the stalk end. Botrytis may be controlled by spraying the flowers—not the fruit—with captan or Elvaron, but commonsense management ensuring plenty of light and air is at least as effective. In theory, the strawberries least likely to suffer from botrytis are those grown in barrels (Chapter 6).

Virus diseases once nearly destroyed the strawberry industry in this country but the amateur who buys certified plants from a reputable firm has nothing to worry about. One must be careful, though, over new introductions which have not received certification, be they advertised as 'monsters', 'novelties', 'climbers' or whatever.

Raspberries. Buy certified canes as insurance against Mosaic virus. The raspberry beetle, referred to in our general survey of pests, is controlled by spraying with derris ten days after flowering with a repeat dose ten days after that. Unless you have actually had maggotty raspberries the previous year don't worry.

A lot of raspberries and loganberries are lost from mould when ripe. Pick frequently and thoroughly; one over-ripe berry left in a cluster will grow 'whiskers' and infect the others. Pick dry if possible, but if damp berries are unavoidable don't leave them in a punnet. Empty into a dish and sprinkle at once with caster sugar, or spread very thinly and place in the bottom of the 'frige.

CHAPTER THREE
Vegetables

BROAD BEANS

BROCCOLI: PURPLE SPROUTING: CALABRESSE

FRENCH BEANS

GLOBE ARTICHOKES

MARROWS AND COURGETTES

MELONS

PEAS: ASPARAGUS PEAS: SUGAR PEAS

RUNNER BEANS

SEAKALE BEET

SPINACH: NEW ZEALAND SPINACH: SPINACH BEET

SQUASHES

SWEET CORN

Vegetables

Three sorts of veg. are entitled to living-space in the very small garden; (1) Those difficult and/or expensive to buy. (2) Those which suffer most in transit from grower to consumer. (3) Those giving a maximum yield from a small area. Globe artichokes and seakale beet would come in the first category; sweet corn and sprouting broccoli in the second; runner and climbing French beans in the last.

Root vegetables and cabbages travel well and are practically always on tap at reasonable prices, so the selective gardener buys them. The same applies to green peas, which keep their flavour when frozen. Frozen broad beans, on the other hand, are a poor substitute for the real thing, and the fresh ones are often hard to find young and unwilted—in which state they are worth anyone's attention. Marrows are cheap and plentiful by August, but the small early ones are neither. The far superior squashes, now supplanting the marrow in the United States, can hardly be bought anywhere in this country.

Mention of squashes suggests one more criterion in our choice of vegetables: we like some of them to be both interesting and decorative.

BROAD BEANS

Not everyone likes this vegetable, and its better-known varieties are unsuitable where space is precious. This is a pity, for it is richer in protein than any of our common vegetables, and is well supplied with carbohydrates and with three of the main vitamins. Like all the legumes it enriches the soil with the nitrogen-forming bacteria of its roots, and the honeysuckle scent of the smallest bean row on a warm, still evening is the most countryfied smell the town garden can produce. The quality of broad beans deteriorates rapidly after picking, so I suggest sampling the fresh product by growing a limited batch of one of the miniature forms.

Soil and Cultivation. A naturally heavy soil, dug during the winter and in reasonably good heart, will need no special preparation. Lighter soils will benefit from rather more compost, and on them broad beans can be sown earlier to mature before conditions become too dry and hot for their liking.

First sowing on light soil can be in February, but in most gardens the surface will not be dry enough until March. Tall-growing broad beans are usually sown in a double row but the dwarf varieties recommended here are best in a single row owing to their spreading habit. Seed is spaced at 4 in. and not more than $1\frac{1}{2}$ in. deep for early sowings though a little deeper later on (soil is warmest near the surface in spring). Keep a look-out for mice and set traps if they are seen to be digging the beans up. Otherwise there's not much to worry about; birds won't touch broad beans and moderate spring frosts never harm them. Later, when the plants are in bloom, the black aphids may appear and will have to be dealt with. Pick out the tips of all those branches carrying a good show of bloom and burn them. This deprives the aphids of their main base and also encourages the setting and swelling of the pods. If you *have* to use an insecticide spray weekly with pyrethrum from mid-May.

Varieties. The Sutton, Midget, and Dwarf Fan. The first is the oldest of the type—and only six years old at that—and still probably the best. The pods contain up to five beans, smaller than ordinary commercial ones and very good eating.

One last point: when the beans are finished don't pull them up, cut off the tops and leave the roots to decay in the soil.

BROCCOLI

Not the sort generally called cauliflowers, which are too large and unreliable for the small garden, but the sprouting broccoli. As a personal choice I would swap all the other brassicas for them on grounds of flavour and value for space occupied. A great many pickings may be had from six good plants and an area of just 9 ft. by 18 in.

Of the two main types, one crops in early spring and the other in early autumn.

Purple Sprouting Broccoli. This is usually on sale from March onwards, but is often marketed with a lot of large leaves and hard stems to make up the weight. The tender sprouts of the home-grown product are very different.

As purple sprouting has to stand the winter the plants are better not to be too large and soft. So don't give any special manurial treatment and don't plant too early in the summer. Mid-July is a convenient time, a piece of ground vacated by an early crop often being available by then. Your garden shop should stock plants, but make enquiries in advance as they are usually less plentiful than other members of the cabbage family. Puddle the plants in and see that they don't dry out in the first fortnight. Thereafter they need no attention but an occasional hoeing. Planting distance is 18 in.

Seed may be sown in permanent positions, and this sometimes gives better results than transplanting. Take out a $\frac{1}{2}$ in. deep drill, drop a tiny pinch of seed every 18 in., cover, and firm the surface. To protect from birds, black cotton the row immediately—the seedlings should be up in a week. Late June is a good time to sow, but a few weeks either way doesn't matter.

Purple sprouting needs no winter protection, especially in a town garden, but any decaying leaves should be removed. When the flower shoots appear from the leaf axils in spring pick them while small and tender. Picking continues over several weeks and the young leaves may be cooked with the shoots.

There are no very distinct varieties, though labels such as Early and Extra Early may have some basis in fact. White Sprouting Broccoli is obtainable but the flavour is no improvement on that of the purple variety and it lacks the latter's attractive deep green colour when cooked.

Calabresse. This Italian green sprouting broccoli has become more popular here since the deep-freezers took it up. It comes into use in late summer just when one is getting bored with peas and beans, but being tender it must be finished before the frosts come in November.

Culture is exactly as for purple sprouting, but since it has to grow quickly and not stand the winter it can do with more feeding. A high-nitrogen organic, dried blood or fish manure, may be raked in before sowing, which is best done during May. Like all brassicas calabresse and purple sprouting prefer slighly alkaline soils, so if you suspect yours of acidity give it a dressing of hydrated lime or ground limestone, 8 oz. per sq. yd., during the winter.

The dwarf French bean produces a much smaller crop in relation to surface area occupied than does the runner bean, and so is less satisfactory for the small garden. On light sandy soils, however, the French bean will do well under drought conditions which runners cannot tolerate. Some people prefer the French bean to eat, so if your soil and/or your palate incline you towards it why not try the climbing varieties instead of the familiar dwarf?

Cultivation. Heavy soils need a winter dressing of compost during digging, and texture will be improved by an application of hydrated lime at 8 oz. per sq. yd. Light soils may also benefit from this limeing because French beans can stand a poor soil but not an acid one.

Sowing in the open may be possible at the end of April, but nothing is gained by attempting it while the ground is still cold and wet. A single row may be sown, or a double staggered one in a wide drill (see Runner Beans) according to the type of support up which the beans are to climb. French gardeners have a saying to the effect that these beans, when sown, should be able to see the gardener even though he cannot see them. In other words they must not be sown too deeply if poor germination, rotting seed and distorted seed leaves are to be avoided. Under cloches, sowing can be in mid-April if the site has been cloched for at least a week previously to warm the soil. Space at about 4 in. apart and always sow a few extra for 'gapping up'. When buying seed get a quarter-pint packet if possible, a half-pint is usually too much for a small garden.

Staking. Less of a problem than it is with the taller growing and heavier cropping runners. Light or medium bamboos 5 ft. long, Weldmesh or Gro-mesh netting on angle-irons, lengths of twine attached to a wooden fence, anything that is stable and slender enough for the vines to encircle will do. The maximum height will not have to be more than 5 ft.

Varieties. Earliest Of All is similar to most of the dwarf types. Blue Lake White Seeded is one of the round podded stringless varieties popular in America. Purple Podded and Blue Coco have rather decorative bluish pods which turn green in cooking. Both are stringless and of good quality.

This bulky and somewhat unproductive object may seem a curious choice, but if you happen to like it—and some people are positively addicted—an attempt is not unreasonable. It is a luxury (and always has been; Pliny the Elder said it was the dearest Roman vegetable), it is a handsome specimen plant and could be dotted among perennials or shrubs, and, finally, a town environment may suit it. I say that because so many artichokes die during the winter in spite of efforts to protect them, and the hardest frosts are rarely experienced in urban areas.

Cultivation. Forget all about the globe artichoke if you have to garden in a cold Northern or Eastern district or on a badly drained clay. In the South, even a light soil needs deep cultivation to break up any hard 'pan' of subsoil. Get the tines of a fork down below the usual digging depth and lever them from side to side; don't bring the subsoil to the surface. Turn a good bucketful of compost or manure into the soil of each intended planting station and leave rough for at least part of the winter.

Order plants from a nursery for delivery in April, plant immediately on arrival, and pamper them a bit through their first summer with occasional feeds of liquid manure. Pick off any flower buds as soon as you see them—no crop for the first year. When the leaves die down in autumn protect the crowns with a light covering of straw or sedge peat. Rake this off in March and fork gently round the plants. The first heads will be cut that summer.

The parent plants will crop for several years. Propagate by taking the suckers or offsets which develop round the crown and planting them in spring. Six plants are generally reckoned to produce enough heads for the average family, but in view of their size you are unlikely to find room for this number. They should be spaced 4 ft. apart if grown in a row and need an equivalent space if grown as specimen plants in border or shrubbery. In this situation, though, they can be as ornamental as the Globe Thistle (*Echinops Ritro*) and a good deal more so than a weatherbeaten yucca.

The vegetable marrow has been described as a piece of clotted water with a strong flavour of nothing. The courgette is an infantile marrow, and at 15p a pound one of the most over-priced vegetables on the market. The American squashes are more worth growing, but many good cooks clamour for marrows, no doubt looking upon them as a challenge to their art.

For the small gardener the marrow has something to be said for it. The bush varieties will fill an unused corner; the trailers will do a cover-up job if you have something nasty outside the wood-shed; there is a tropical lushness about the flamboyant yellow flowers.

Soil and Cultivation. Whatever you may think of chemical fertilizers, one thing is certain: you will never grow good marrows with them. Not even the commercial growers feed them with what the old farm-hands used contemptuously to label 'bag-muck'. Like all the Cucurbitae, marrows must have a soil rich in humus.

For each plant take out a hole a foot deep and 18 in. square, then replace the soil, mixing it with well-rotted compost, peat, municipal compost or anything of the sort. Chop it well into the soil during the refilling: the marrow plant will not appreciate a sandwich with a solid compost filling between two layers of poor soil. Leave the surface of each station as a gently rounded hump.

Sowing. For sowing in the open, allow three seeds to each prepared station. If the soil is lumpy scrape a little away and replace it with a handful of compost, then push the seeds in, point first, until just covered. Keep moist, and put a protective ring of slug pellets round each station a week after sowing—neglect of this simple precaution has cost me scores of marrow plants in the seed-leaf stage.

If cloches are available, sowing can take place in mid-April, otherwise late May is early enough. Even then, be ready to pop a flower pot over the seedlings on cold nights. Reduce them to one per station when the first rough leaves have developed.

Pot-raised marrows react badly to root disturbance. Sow if possible in peat pots in early May, the plants are ready for setting out in four weeks when grown in a cold greenhouse;

too early a start often results in their being starved and yellow through waiting weeks for favourable weather.

Fertilization. Female flowers are carried on the tips of baby marrows; they must be fertilized or the babies will not develop. There is usually a large surplus of male blooms but not always enough insects to transfer the pollen, so hand pollination is worthwhile. Pick a recently opened male bloom, strip off the petals and push the stamens into the female flower, leaving them there in contact with the stigma.

Surplus male flowers need not be wasted. They can be dipped in batter, fried in oil for five minutes, and served as rather exotic fritters.

Varieties. The best early bush type is Zucchini, a dark green marrow with a compact habit which can be grown to full size or cut small for use as courgettes. In the United States these tiny fruits are known as fingerlings, a fair guide to the size at which they are harvested. Zucchini is an excellent cloche variety and may be planted only 2 ft. apart. It develops greyish markings on the leaves which are sometimes mistaken for mildew but are in fact natural and healthy.

One of the best trailers is Table Dainty; plants go on fruiting for a long time if the fruits are kept cut. They are small and of good quality. If your interest is solely in courgettes use the true Continental Courgette instead of baby marrows. It is bred for the purpose and just as easy to grow.

MELONS

All right, so melons are really fruit. The point is that they are grown like vegetables and were at one time thought of as a superior pumpkin. Tudor gardeners classified pumpkins as 'milions' and what we call melons as 'musk milions'. Of course, they differ not only in the character of the fruit but in the degree of tenderness of the plants. Quality melons of the greenhouse varieties are not for the amateur, though some of the less demanding sort are considered in Chapter 5. Here we are concerned with the half-hardy cantaloupe hybrids which can be grown under cloches.

Cultivation. Soil preparation should be as for marrows or cucumbers with the digging in of any humus-forming material as the first priority. A sheltered sunny corner is the best situation.

Planting out under cloches or in a cold frame is safe by the first week of June. Allow one plant per growers barn cloche or 4 sq. ft. in a cold frame. Put the cloches in position at least a week before planting to warm the soil.

Raising plants in a cold greenhouse is possible from early May, or with a little warmth from late April. If you have no greenhouse the sunny kitchen window-sill is the place. When starting these tender plants in the house the best plan is to group the pots in a polystyrene container. The whole set-up, with peat pots and soil-less compost, is very light and easy to stand outdoors on warm days. Melon seed is more expensive than cucumber or marrow so sow only two per pot. Don't bury the seeds deeply but keep the pots covered with brown paper to prevent drying out between waterings. Reduce to one seedling immediately on germination.

Plant carefully, avoiding root damage. Never allow the plants to lack moisture and surround them with a peat mulch. By midsummer the cloches may need a light smear of white-wash to prevent sunscorch.

Melons can be allowed to grow naturally with the one main stem bearing the fruit, but under cloches it is better to stop them when they have about four leaves, to produce laterals. Keep only two of these laterals, and stop them too when they carry not more than two swelling fruits each. Really, these plants should bear only two or three melons. If a lot of un-wanted side-shoots overcrowd the cloches be ruthless with them. Pollination of the female flowers should take place naturally, but if you find the baby fruit are dying off instead of swelling fertilize the female flowers by hand as described for marrows.

Rest the young melons on pieces of tile or wads of folded polythene to make things harder for slugs, and give the plants a weekly drink of one of the organic liquid manures. Supply plenty of water until the fruit stops swelling and develops the characteristic ripe melon smell. Then allow the plants gradually to dry off.

Varieties. Sweetheart is among the best of the new F_1 hybrids, with its tolerance of relatively low temperatures and attractive pale green skin and sweet scarlet flesh. It might ripen unprotected in town gardens in the South.

Forget about the ordinary garden pea. You haven't room to grow a worthwhile quantity, and passable supplies are usually on sale in the summer. Frozen peas too are quite edible—and even recognizable as peas. So I would like to introduce a couple of varieties which never get into the shops, the asparagus pea and the sugar pea.

Asparagus Peas. This plant is not really a pea at all, but a lotus. It rejoices in the name of Lotus tetragonolobus, but this should not be held against it. The tiny, fluted pods are produced in great profusion and the plant, bushy and covered with reddish flowers, is interesting and decorative. It requires no staking and can be grown in groups in the flower border or along the edge of a path.

Any average garden soil is good enough and no special manuring is needed. If tests show your soil to be acid a dusting of hydrated lime should be forked in before sowing or planting.

In two respects the species differs completely from the true pea; it is half-hardy, like the runner bean, and it cannot be sown thickly because each plant needs space to bush out. It may be sown under glass in April, three seeds to a peat pot, reduced to one seedling. These are planted out in mid-May, 18 in. apart in groups or rows; this is the best method if you want to integrate it into the flower garden. It may also be sown outdoors in early May, several seeds at 18 in. stations, reduced to the strongest one. Open air sowings should not be more than an inch deep.

Asparagus peas are picked when not more than an inch long and the pod is cooked whole. It becomes tough if left to grow larger, and the continuous picking of small pods also encourages the plant to go on cropping. The pods are better steamed than boiled (they cook very quickly), and served with melted butter only.

Sugar Peas. This is the French *mange-tout* and is grown like the ordinary garden pea. Winter-dug soil manured with garden compost will ensure a good crop, but again a light dressing of lime should be given if the soil is at all sour. Sow in March or April, quite thickly in wide drills, and at a depth of $1\frac{1}{2}$ in. Where birds are known to be troublesome black cotton should be strung over the rows before germination,

Although the sugar pea is a dwarf the vines may need a little support. Horizontal strings along both sides of the row. attached to 18 in. high pegs, will keep them clear of the ground.

The pods are picked while still quite flat and cooked whole. Use them as soon as possible after picking.

Varieties. Asparagus Pea, Sweetgreen, Carouby de Maussan.

RUNNER BEANS

Even where your gardening space is restricted horizontally there will be unlimited room vertically. Runner beans are a good way to make use of it if you have a patch of soil for a base.

This book mentions several edible crops which do not detract from the appearance of a mainly decorative garden, but the runner bean is unique among them in being originally grown purely as an ornament. It came to England from South America in the seventeenth century and hardly anyone thought of eating it for more than a hundred years. Philips, in his *History of Cultivated Vegetables* (1821), says he can remember it being grown 'as an ornament to cover walls and to form arbours, without any idea of cooking the pods for table'. A dual-purpose role would seem more sensible.

Soil. As good as you can make it. Dig in garden compost, municipal compost, processed sludge, hop manure—any bulky organic stuff—during the winter. Leave the ground rough to weather down to a kindly tilth. This preparation is essential whether you intend a full-scale bean row or isolated groups. A week or two before sowing or planting incorporate a 4 oz. per sq. yd. dressing of fish manure or dried blood in the top few inches.

Sowing. About May 10th in the open, in a drill 6 in. wide if you are growing a row. A double row is sown in staggered formation, the seed spaced at 4 in. in the rows and the rows by the full width of the drill. The double row of plants is intended for a double row of sticks or bamboos, the neatest form of support. Sow at least a dozen extra seeds at one end of the drill to provide spare plants for filling gaps. With good germination you should have two or three plants to each stick, but they are quite happy with that situation. Don't cover the seed with more than 1 in. of soil.

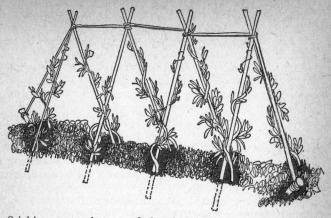

Sticking runner beans. 7 ft. bamboos, 6 in. in ground. Twine looped round intersections and strained to pegs at both ends.

Under cloches sowing is possible in mid-April and you will pick beans much earlier. Leave the cloches on until they reach the glass, then de-cloche and stick immediately. Don't let the vines grow through the gaps in the roof-glass or they will get damaged.

When sowing in positions where a drill is not practicable the seed may be simply pushed an inch below the surface and the soil levelled. Or plants may be raised in greenhouse or cold frame and put out in late May. The runner is tolerant of transplanting and seeds may be sown 2 in. apart in a seed tray of potting compost, though better results and an absence of any check are obtained from single plants raised in peat pots of the Jiffy Pot type.

Cultivation and Staking. Runners must have moisture or the pods will neither set nor swell. Apart from watering, the most effective measure is a mulch of compost or sedge peat extending at least 18 in. from the plants. Not only will this conserve moisture, it will prevent the soil being compacted by all the treading it gets during picking—and it will keep the picker's shoes clean.

Runners may be grown in dwarf form by repeatedly stopping the leading shoots, but in bad weather the pods tend to drag on the ground and become distorted and sluggy and the plants anything but decorative. To look nice and crop well the runner should be allowed to behave naturally and run. Staking must provide a firm support because a rock-a-bye-baby act in high winds can be disastrous. That is why I am against the use of flexible netting unless it can be tautly erected on strong stakes, one sees too many instances of unhappy-looking beans clinging to sagging, waving, netting. And removing the dead growth from the stuff in the autumn drives all but the most patient round the twist.

The most adaptable stake is the 7 ft. bamboo. Taken up when the crop finishes and stored in the dry these canes last for years. For staking a double row they are inserted 1 ft. apart along both sides at least 3 in. outside the plants, and then brought together so that their tops cross above the centre of the row. They are tied in this position by a continuous strand of stout garden twine passing round the point where they cross. A length of this twine is left hanging at each end of the row to be attached to a stout peg or angle iron driven in 2 ft. from the last cane. The string is strained tight to act as a stay in keeping the whole structure neat and rigid. For isolated groups use four canes in a 'teepee' shape, the four corners of a square, brought together at the top and tied. Two or three bean plants can be allowed to each cane. For covering a fence or wall a single row of canes can be used, again kept from lurching out of place by a string passing round each and tethered to the wall at both ends. A more permanent and expensive arrangement is 'Gro-Mesh' rigid metal-and-plastic netting, which is held clear of the wall by special fixing brackets.

Varieties. Old favourites like Prizewinner and Streamline are completely reliable. Among the newcomers Sutton's Enorma (syn. Twenty-one) seems to have everything. For an early maturing variety choose Kelvedon Marvel. A very interesting one is White Wonder; the flowers are white, the pods long and almost stringless, and any which get too old to use can be allowed to ripen their beans which are also white and can be used as butter beans. The non-trailing Hammond's Dwarf Scarlet is generally recommended for small gardens and for cloche growing, but I have not been impressed by its cropping powers.

It ought to be better known. It will grow on heavy soils, its appearance is such that one seedsman suggests using it as a foliage plant in flower beds, and it's delicious to eat.

The part eaten is the leaf stalk and the midrib of the leaf. The deep green crinkled leaves grow in an erect cluster and the white stalks and midribs can be 2 or 3 in. wide. As they are cut more are thrown up.

Cultivation and Soil. A heavy soil enriched with compost and weathered to a good tilth is the best basis. This would be improved by a sprinkling of dried blood or hoof-and-horn raked in before sowing, and the plants would be further helped by a weekly drink of Bio or similar liquid when in full growth. Nitrogen is needed to produce leaf, and the more luxuriant the foliage the better it looks and tastes.

Sow in April in 1 in. deep drills and thin to a foot apart. Sowing in stations at that distance, five or six seeds to a station thinned to one, will save time and seed. Plants dotted about a flower border are also sown in this way; soil is scooped away with a trowel, a few seeds dropped, and the soil replaced. The sowings are marked with pegs or labels. Seakale beet cannot be transplanted.

Using the Crop. The leaves are cut at ground level when they are about 15 in. tall. The whole of the leaf stalk and the white rib through the middle of the leaf are used. Normally the largest leaves are used and the remainder left to grow. The green part of the leaf is very good cooked as spinach, but there is not usually enough of it to be worth cooking.

Cooking is not my province, but the standard advice to cut up the stems of seakale beet and boil in water with a squeeze of lemon to keep them white is no way to win new friends for this vegetable. The stems should be steamed whole until tender and served covered with melted butter. Obviously, the flavour is supposed to be that of seakale, but I would put it closer to asparagus.

Varieties. There is a red one called Rhubarb Chard, even more decorative then the white form and recommended for flower arrangement in addition to its primary function. The white variety may be listed as Seakale Beet, Silver Beet, or Swiss Chard. One word of warning: if you try to buy the seed at a garden shop and they are out of stock don't be conned into believing that Spinach Beet is 'exactly the same'. It's quite different and we shall consider it under 'Spinach'.

SPINACH

I'm no spinach fan—indeed, I would go along with an old friend who assured me that he would never bother with it while he could get a helping of green slime from the nearest pond. This, of course, is purest prejudice. Most people like spinach and some prefer it to any other green vegetable. Nutritionally, it is a rich source of vitamins and minerals.

One difficulty in writing about spinach is that it is a portmanteau description of several completely different plants which just happen to produce edible green leaves. The three main sorts are treated in different ways.

Summer or Round Seeded Spinach. The kind most usually found in the shops, and the least satisfactory choice for the very small garden. It takes up a lot of room—every cook knows that a considerable bulk is needed for a modest end result—it requires generous treatment, and on light sandy soils it's a dead loss. It does however tolerate more shade than most vegetables.

Soil for spinach must have plenty of decayed organic matter in it, preferably compost applied during winter cultivation. Digging in the spring not only makes a tilth more difficult to obtain but accelerates the loss of soil moisture, which is the one thing you don't want for summer spinach. To boost the available nitrogen a dressing of dried blood or fish meal should be lightly forked in a week before sowing.

Sow in a wide drill, evenly and fairly thinly. Mid-March is early enough even in the South. When the seedlings are tall enough to have developed a few good leaves thin them to 6 in. apart. Snip the roots off the thinnings and use them. Thereafter keep the crop well watered and finish it up as soon as it runs to seed. A later sowing can be made on the same site.

New Zealand Spinach. This is the only summer variety to grow on poor soils. It is a half-hardy annual which trails about the ground rather like ivy. The leaves are fleshy and have the general appearance of a succulent. Flavour is rated by spinach addicts as inferior to that of other varieties, but the yield of leaves and shoots from even a few plants is considerable.

Although N.Z. spinach will crop on poor soil it naturally responds to the same treatment as the summer variety, and an occasional good soaking in dry weather, though not essential, will not be wasted. It may be sown under glass and planted out in early June like any other half-hardy, but an outdoor sowing in mid-May is the most practicable.

Sow on stations at least 2 ft. apart. Give each station a little pocket of really good soil or compost, sow a sprinkling of seed—about six—at each, cover $\frac{1}{2}$ in. deep, and keep moist. Thin eventually to one per station, but don't be in too much of a hurry to do this. If the seedlings start disappearing suspect slugs and put down slug bait. Weeding is important at first, but a vigorous mature specimen can smother most opposition.

Spinach Beet. The most valuable of the three. It can be used all the year round, especially if you can spare it some cloches in the winter. It will put up with most soils and I have seen it growing on raw London clay thoughtfully spread around by builders in a new garden.

For summer and autumn use, sow in April; for winter, in July. The spring sowing *may* last into the winter, but because it is so useful at that time it is better to rely on a batch started later.

Any compost, wood ash or weathered soot you can spare is best dug in during the winter. Given a chance, the plant develops a powerful root system, and the more thorough your winter digging the quicker it is able to do so.

Sow in 1 in. deep drills, dropping a few seeds every 8 in. Thin these to one at each station. It may be necessary to string black cotton along the rows, birds like the seedlings in summer and will peck the leaves in winter. If you intend to cover the winter crop with growers barn cloches the July sowing should be of two rows 1 ft. apart. Cloche them in October and keep the leaves closely picked. In hard frost the plants will die down, but new growth appears with the lengthening days. They survive quite well without cloching, but even in a sheltered town garden you will have less winter spinach than when protection can be given.

Spinach beet probably produces more fresh greens per square foot than any other vegetable.

Varieties. Summer spinach: Long Standing Round. New Zealand spinach: Cut and Come Again. Spinach beet may be listed as Perpetual Spinach. (Not to be confused with Seakale Beet).

SQUASHES

Squash is an American word for various members of the marrow and pumpkin family. The Red Indians called them *askutasquash* ('eaten raw'), but this has been mercifully shortened. Another improvement is that we now cook them.

The squashes are more worth growing than marrows. Their flesh is less watery, better flavoured, and has a higher carbohydrate content. In the small garden they can be trained up fences, trellis, poles or netting, and some are quite decorative. Several varieties, if allowed to ripen on the vine, will keep for months and help with winter menus.

Cultivation is exactly as for marrows, which see. Training the right sorts on trellis or bean netting is easy as the leading shoots are woven in and out of the mesh, but on other forms of support the vines should be frequently tied. Remember that even the smaller types are solid and heavy and a well-grown Hubbard Squash can weigh 10 lb.

Varieties. The two best for use in the winter are Hubbard and Butternut. The first is like a very heavy deep green Rugby football. The skin becomes iron hard and the flesh is orange in colour. Hubbard is a good keeper and a good cropper, one autumn I filled a 2 cwt. corn bin with the produce of three plants. Butternut is smaller, bottle-shaped, and when ripe perhaps the best flavoured of the entire family. Both are trailers and as easy to grow as the common marrow.

For use in the summer try Vegetable Spaghetti or the American favourite, Baby Crookneck. The latter is a bush variety but compact enough to merit the trial of a couple of plants. The fruit is a better proposition than the average courgette.

There are dozens of squashes and a selection will be found in most catalogues. But don't grow Ornamental Gourds in the belief that they are edible.

SWEET CORN

The growing of sweet corn in this country has become less of a gamble with the introduction of hybrids suited to our climate. It may seem an unsuitably large choice for the small garden, but a group of sweet corn, with its long drooping leaves and tall tassels of male flowers, has a decorative value all its own for the back of a flower border or as a quick-growing screen. Incidentally, it should always be planted in blocks or groups rather than single-file rows; it is wind-fertilized and in a row the pollen from the tassel may be blown away instead of settling on the female 'silk' of the cobs.

Soil and Situation. Plenty of sun is vital, but some shelter from strong wind is also an advantage. For this reason sweet corn may do better in a small enclosed garden with a South aspect than in a more open space. The higher night temperatures of an urban garden compared with a country one can add a useful week or so to its growing season.

Like most forms of maize sweet corn will produce a crop of sorts on almost any soil, given warmth and moisture. For good quality cobs, though, it must have organic materials within reach of its rather shallow roots. A pailful of peat per square yard mixed with the topsoil before planting or sowing, plus a peat mulch when the plants are established, will take care of this.

Planting. Seed may be sown in the open in May, 1 in. deep, on stations spaced 1 by 2 ft. Sow three seeds per station and thin to one. Cloches are an invaluable protection against both birds and frost.

Sweet corn may also be raised in pots for planting out about the third week of May. Sow in Levington Potting or JI No. 1 at the end of April in unheated greenhouse, cold frame, or light window-sill. Use 3 in. pots or peat pots and sow three seeds to a pot, reducing to one seedling on germination. Sweet corn's roots are few and fleshy and hate disturbance, but the use of peat pots and the light soil-less composts will minimize this trouble. Pot-raised plants are more satisfactory than direct sowing in colder districts and where groups are to be grown in the flower garden.

Cultivation and Harvesting. Watering may be neccessary, but the peat mulch, applied when the soil is moist, will reduce its frequency. If the plants are affected by wind soil should be drawn up around the stems; adventitious roots will grow out into it from the buds near the soil surface.

Cobs should be ready about six weeks after the appearance of the 'silk'. Test by extracting a few grains and squeezing them. When just right the contents are of the consistency of clotted cream; too soon, they will still be watery; too late, and they will be doughy, with much of the sugar converted into starch. This transition to starchiness goes on rapidly even after the cob is harvested and probably has much to do with complaints about the quality of sweet corn on sale. It needs to be gathered at the right stage and cooked with the least possible delay.

Varieties. North of a line Liverpool to The Wash: North Star, John Innes Hybrid. South of the line: Earliking, Kelvedon Glory, and Sutton's First Of All, plus the above two.

At the time of writing, the new variety Honey Dew has given outstanding trial results. Look out for it in the catalogues.

CHAPTER FOUR

Salad Crops

AMERICAN LAND CRESS

CELTUCE

CHICORY

CUCUMBERS OUTDOORS

DANDELIONS

ENDIVE

LETTUCE

LAMBS LETTUCE

RADISHES

SPRING ONIONS

TOMATOES

Salad Crops

The British salad *is* improving—slowly. There is more willingness to experiment and a less total reliance on flabby lettuce with minor trimmings. Things would be better still if a greater variety of ingredients were available, but you won't find celtuce or dandelions or Continental tomatoes in the average greengrocer's.

Other reasons for growing your own salads—even lettuce —have to do with condition and price. By their very nature salad crops are highly perishable, and that indefinable thing, 'freshness', is easily lost in marketing. It is lost most quickly in hot summer weather, at the very time when the law of supply and demand is most loaded against the buyer. That is why price so often rockets as quality plummets.

From the housekeeping viewpoint even a small plot devoted to salads is worthwhile. And things like the new hybrid cucumbers have a real gardening interest.

AMERICAN LAND CRESS

This was widely grown at one time and as it still appears in the major seed catalogues some people are evidently faithful to it. It's a straggly sort of plant which at its best is a good substitute for watercress.

Cultivation. American cress (the name is a misnomer, it is a European native) is most useful as a winter salad. Very severe weather will destroy it, but in a town garden it should survive long enough to give pickings at times when watercress is short.

Sowings may be made as early as April and the plants will be usable in two to three months. For winter use the main sowing is in August. The leaves and shoots will be more tender and prolific if the soil contains plenty of compost or even peat. This is as much a matter of maintaining moisture as of providing nutriment. American cress must never be allowed to get too dry; it will also grow in shade, which is one of its advantages.

87

Seed is sown in shallow drills and if the tilth is good it may be sown thinly enough to grow on without further thinning. Keep weeds down in its early stages—the stuff has a weedlike look, so be careful not to hoe or pull it up.

Young shoots, which are what you want, are encouraged by persistent picking and by cutting back overgrown plants.

MUSTARD AND CRESS (see Chapter 6)

CELTUCE

Although easy to grow, celtuce has never caught on among gardeners. Its obviously synthetic name, compounded of celery and lettuce, suggests something phoney. Really it's a useful summer salad, part of which may also be served as a cooked vegetable. It has a less aggressive flavour than celery, for which its heart or central stem is a substitute, and its outer leaves are a welcome change from lettuce. From the dietetic point of view it scores over lettuce, having four times the latter's vitamin C content. The celery-like heart is excellent both raw and cooked.

Cultivation is exactly the same as for summer lettuce (see p. 94). The first sowing should not be made until April, for quality depends a lot on uninterrupted growth. Give the plants plenty of room, thinning to at least 8 in., and water in dry weather.

It would be as well to try only a small sowing if celtuce is new to you, but in subsequent years you may decide on successional sowings. For a continuous succession a sowing every three weeks would be neccessary, for the plant does not 'stand' in good condition long in hot weather. The last sowing should be made at the end of June.

There are no separate varieties of celtuce. Not all seedmen stock it, but Thompson and Morgan offer it at about 12½p a packet.

CHICORY

If this health-giving winter salad has become better known lately the credit must be given to the Belgians. They have backed their exports of it to this country with persistent advertising, and the creamy white heads are now a familiar sight in the greengrocer's.

The amateur's product will probably be smaller and looser-leaved than these, but fresher and crisper. We really ought to grow our own chicory because it grows wild in Britain; I have seen its tall stems and starry sky-blue flowers brightening a disused chalk-pit.

Cultivation. Chicory is a biennial, like the Sweet William. It starts from seed one year and comes to maturity the following year. The part used in salads is really the beginning of the second year's growth, started in darkness in the winter and cut before the leaves begin to unfold.

Seed is sown from April to June in shallow drills 9 in. apart and the seedlings thinned to the same distance. Seed is cheap and germination good, but don't let the plants remain crowded. Even with this spacing you can fit about sixty of them in a space measuring 6 by 3 ft., and you want them to grow well and make a good root.

Chicory is a lime-lover and if your soil is at all acid a good dusting of hydrated lime should be worked in before sowing. Very poor or very heavy soil should have some compost or hop manure, but in a fair average soil no special treatment is needed. An occasional good soaking in dry spells, a peat mulch if possible, and the immediate cutting of any flower heads that appear, sum up the growing season's work. On that last point, you will get more of these bolters when you sow early—June sowings are less likely to run to seed.

Blanching. When growth dies down the roots may be lifted, very small ones thrown away, and the rest covered with soil or a good layer of peat in a shallow trench. Or they may be left where grown and lifted as required. In either case the roots should be damaged as little as possible and the dead foliage cut off well above the crown.

Any deep enough container may be used for forcing, a 10 in. pot, a box, or a plastic bucket. Pack the roots in tightly with their tops about level, then sift fine soil or compost down between them, leaving the crowns just clear of its surface. Levington Compost may be used for the sake of lightness, it can be used again for the next batch. Watering should aim at keeping it only just moist.

A dark cupboard with a temperature of 50°F. or over is the ideal forcing spot, but any frost-free shed, garage or cellar will do. The lower the temperature the slower the growth but the really important thing is absolute darkness. Gleams of daylight will spoil the colour of the 'chicons' and make them bitter.

Variety: Witloof.

CUCUMBERS OUTDOORS

The cucumber has been popular for a long time. *Like a booth in a vineyard*, says the Prophet Isaiah, *like a lodge in a cucumber field*. Not everyone can eat cucumbers with impunity, but some who find the greenhouse varieties indigestible claim that they suffer no ill-effects from eating the open-air kinds. There would appear to be no logical reason for this, but I've heard it too often to dismiss it entirely.

Trailers and Climbers. Outdoor varieties used to be called Ridge Cucumbers, because they were grown like marrows on heaps of rotted manure. This is no longer practicable for most gardeners, but cucumbers still need a soil rich in organic matter and prefer a slightly raised bed to ensure good drainage.

Plants are put out during the first half of June, each on a low mound of soil and compost. Don't plant too deeply or you may have trouble with stem rot, the seed leaves should be well above the surface. Where the plants are to trail on the ground they should be spaced 3 ft. apart and stopped at six leaves to develop laterals. The ground should be mulched with peat to discourage weeds and keep the cucumbers clean. The new climbing varieties are planted 18 in. apart close to a permanent fence or trellis or a temporary support of bamboos. Contrary to what one is sometimes told, they are not good natural climbers and the main stem must be tied with soft string or fillis as it goes up, being stopped when it reaches the top of the support to encourage the development of laterals. These side-growths are also tied to the supporting framework and will carry most of the crop. Cut the cucumbers as soon as they reach reasonable size and don't let the plants cry out. Any sort of mulch is good and so is a liquid organic feed given weekly from the swelling of the first fruits.

Raising Plants. Seed may be sown direct out of doors in late May and covered with cloches or even jam jars, but pot-grown plants sown indoors in the first week of May will do better. This can be done in greenhouse, cold frame, or a good light window-sill. Use 3 in. pots filled to within an inch of the top with J.I. No. 2 or Levington Potting (not a seed compost). Push three seeds edgeways into this and cover with another ½ in. of compost. Keep moist and find a warm spot for germination. Leave only one plant in each pot—it's better to throw some away than to be left with empty pots through erratic germination. Never allow the little plants to dry out.

Growing under Cloches. Outdoor varieties do well under cloches and I have also had good results from the cold greenhouse variety Conqueror. Planting is safe a fortnight earlier than in the open. Adequate watering is essential, and the cloches should be lightly coated with limewash to prevent scorching.

Varieties. Bedfordshire Ridge, Kaga, Kyoto, Burpee Hybrid, Nadir, Baton Vert. The last four are recommended for climbing. Baton Vert failed completely on my heavy ground, but that was probably the result of poor drainage in a wet summer. Reverting to the question of digestibility, the variety Burpless, introduced in the U.S. under the slogan 'Not a burp in a bushel' is now available here. It grows well outdoors, you eat it skin and all, and it's rich in vitamins.

DANDELIONS

If you have a scruffy corner where wild ones grow you might as well clean it up and grow tame ones. As long ago as 1938 that great expert on vegetables, Eleanour Sinclair Rohde, was claiming that nurserymen and food reformers would end our neglect of the dandelion, but so far I have never seen it offered for sale. In France it is used primarily as an early spring salad in competition with endive and chicory, being blanched in the same way.

Cultivation. Exactly as for chicory. As might be expected, the dandelion is unfussy as to soil. It won't matter if a few plants come into bloom so if space is available you can sow in April.

It is hardly worth lifting the roots for blanching, though in this too they may be treated just like chicory. It's simpler to cover them with pots or boxes, or a strip of black polythene anchored round the edges with soil, when growth starts in early spring. The cover must be really light-tight—remember to plug the drainage holes if you use inverted flower pots.

The leaves will grow in an off-white rosette which will add

a speculative interest to the dullest salad. I have never grown the cultivated form, but have blanched wild dandelions in a year of greenstuff shortage and rated them higher than purchased endive. Dandelion leaves and roots are credited with all sorts of medicinal virtues on which I am not competent to judge, but the plant is certainly rich in minerals like all those with long tap-roots.

The cultivated variety is Thick Leaved. It is not a widely stocked seed but some garden shops and centres now offer Continental varieties and they should supply it. You can also get it from Dobies of Chester (ask for their special list, 'Vegetables for Epicures').

ENDIVE

People sometimes confuse it with chicory, but its yellowish leafy or curly appearance is very different from that of the latter's smooth ivory heads. However, both belong to the genus *Cichorium*, and both have been cultivated for more than 2,000 years. In this country, it is mentioned in a book in 1618, and a bit later Parkinson listed it as 'much used in winter as a sallet herbe with greate delight'.

Soil and Cultivation. Endive is essentially a plant for light, rich soils. The ideal would be a sandy loam enriched with compost or processed sludge. On a heavy waterlogged soil the plants will assuredly rot during the autumn. An open sunny position is neccessary for the same reason.

If autumn and winter endive is wanted July is the best month to sow. As with all midsummer sowings you may have to water the seedlings to keep them moving. Rows should be a foot apart and the plants at the same distance after final thinning; they are rather sprawly things and overcrowding sets up decay.

Blanching begins about three months after sowing, the plants being covered with anything that will keep them dry and in the dark. Endive needs about a month in these conditions to lose its green colour and become edible, and the last ones should be covered well before Christmas, when severe weather becomes more likely. The oft-repeated advice that one need only gather the outer leaves of the plant together and tie them round the top like a cos lettuce may have been valid in the Mediterranean countries where endive

92

originated; in our winter climate the end thereof is likely to be a slimy mess.

A recent technique, which I have not seen in operation, is to cloche the crop in early October and to blanch it in these comparatively dry and warm conditions by entirely covering the cloches with black polythene.

Varieties: Curled, Batavian Broad Leaved, Sutton's Winter Lettuce Leaved. The first is the best to eat, the other two the easiest to grow.

LETTUCE

This is still the most important green-leaf basis of salads and likely to remain so for all but the most adventurous. It can be expensive to buy and not always satisfactory when bought, though marketing in polythene bags has made the shop lettuce rather less limp and languid than formerly. But a leafy unhearted lettuce just cut is more flavoursome than a stout-hearted specimen which has been belting along the Hook-Harwich-Covent Garden trail.

There is a confusing variety of lettuce in the catalogues which makes it difficult to know if one is choosing aright. Parkinson was complaining about this in the sixteenth century—'there are so many sorts of Lettice that I doubt I shall scarce be beleeved of a great many'—and he was stuck with fewer than we are. So I shall suggest a short list of personal favourites for each season.

Soil. The lettuce is shallow-rooting and needs moisture-retaining humus in the top 6 in. In poor dry soils it lacks quality and bolts quickly. Compost, peat, hop manure, or processed sludge are all good if worked into the top spit some time before sowing. Where lettuce are to stand the winter try to use ground which has been well treated for a previous crop such as runner beans. Sow in 1 in. deep drills and if the ground is dry water the bottom of the drill before sowing. If birds are known to be troublesome and cloches are not being used protect the seedlings with black cotton, putting it in place *immediately after sowing*. If you wait until the emergent lettuces are visible you will probably never see them at all; birds' eyes are sharper than humans'.

Spring Crops. If cloches are available, sow during the second week of October. Sow fairly thickly in three rows only

6 in. apart. Cloche at once and put end glasses in position. In the event of dry sunny weather the central row may need watering to get it established; otherwise they are left undisturbed during the winter. By February growth will be starting and when the seedlings are 3 in. high you can start to use them for salads, eventually leaving one plant every 9 in., in the two outer rows and pulling the whole of the middle row. You will then be left with the right number of plants, spaced at 9 by 12 in. to grow on to maturity. From eight growers barn cloches you can expect some three dozen hearted lettuce preceded by many handfuls of tender leaves. Varieties: May Queen, Attractie, May Princess.

For wintering outdoors without cloches, sow in September in drills a foot apart and again leave unthinned until spring. Main factors for survival are a well-drained soil, and some protection from birds and the coldest winds. Varieties: Imperial Winter, Arctic King.

Summer and Autumn Crops. Sow from late March to late June. One is always told to sow little and often to ensure a succession, but the later sowings too often get forgotten or the ground they should occupy is pre-empted. It's best to base your succession on a few sowings of different varieties.

In March/April sow equal quantities of Tom Thumb and All The Year Round, either in frame or greenhouse for planting out or *in situ* as soon as soil and weather permit. Tom Thumb, very small and quick-growing, should finish at 6 in. apart in the row, and All The Year Round at 9 in. They will mature at different times.

In April/May sow Continuity, and in May/June, Sutton's Unrivalled. These later sowings must be left to grow where sown and on no account be transplanted. Continuity is an excellent bronze-foliaged lettuce which stands heat and drought without bolting. Unrivalled is a large all-seasons variety which will see you through to autumn.

Cos and Loose-leaf Lettuce. Varieties so far recommended are all cabbage lettuce. Cos are apt to be temperamental, but Sutton's Early Gem, half-way between the two, is small, needs no tying, and can be sown either in spring or in autumn for cloching.

The non-hearting or loose-leaf type is grown like any normal summer variety and its leaves can be plucked and used a few at a time. It is crisp and well flavoured, and is the

94

only lettuce worth growing in window boxes or in pots in the courtyard. Variety: Salad Bowl.

LAMBS LETTUCE

A leading seedsman describes this as the ideal continental winter salad, but my own assessment would be that of Gerard, who long ago classed it in his *Herbal* as being 'none of the worst', adding that although it grew as a weed in this country 'it hath growne in use among the French and Dutch strangers'.

The other name for Lambs Lettuce is Corn Salad, and you may find it so listed in the seed catalogue. It is indeed a native species of arable land and this means that once started in a garden it may continue to reproduce itself as a very inoffensive weed. To make it worth including in your salads, though, it needs fair treatment though not a rich soil.

Cultivation. Sow in August or September for use in autumn and winter, choosing a sunny spot if you can. Sow in drills 6 in. apart or broadcast thinly and cover with fine soil or compost. In either case the seed should be only lightly covered and drills should be no more than $\frac{1}{2}$ in. deep. In dry weather you may have to water regularly to ensure germination, but once the seedlings are up no further attention is needed. A succession of sowings may be made up to the end of September.

Thinnings may be pulled and used and the remaining plants left about 4 in. apart. Leaves from these are gathered as required. In a severe winter they will emerge unscathed from long burial in snow and seem to escape damage by birds and slugs. The flavour is distinctive—rather like that of the wild sorrel that we used to eat as children—and does add interest to the winter salad.

Lambs Lettuce could be grown in a South-facing window-box, and I should think it would winter very well in temporarily vacant sheltered nooks in the rockery, where you might have the satisfaction of asking a friend who knows about alpines to come and identify it for you.

RADISHES

With the exception of mustard and cress, the radish is the quickest-maturing salad. Under the right conditions it is ready for use in a matter of weeks, and a succession can be grown in a very limited space. It has always been a favourite catch crop, sown in odd spaces between rows and even mixed with other vegetables. Old-fashioned gardeners would mix radish with parsley seed; parsley is very slow to germinate and the quick-growing radish marked the position of the row and when pulled for eating would leave the parsley nicely thinned. The same economical use of ground might apply in the flower garden. People invariably leave their hardy annuals in a state of lethal over-population; if some radish seed were mixed in when sowing they would profit by the odd bunch of radish and the annuals would be left with elbow-room to develop properly.

Cultivation. Any good average garden soil will produce tender radishes, failure is usually the gardener's fault and the result of being greedy. Seed is cheap and germinates well; one sows it too thickly and hesitates to decimate the seedlings, hoping that they will all 'come to something'. I've done it myself, and many a time have I been shown a row of solid foliage and asked why the radishes have no bottoms. One tweak with thumb and forefinger will demonstrate a dozen stems crammed so tightly together that the formation of bottoms is physically impossible. Ideally, every radish seed should be sown an inch from every other. Impossible, I know, but that is the sort of spacing to aim at—and it will still give you six large bunches per square foot.

It follows from the above that radishes should not be sown in a narrow drill, but in one made with the full width of a draw hoe. It can run along the edge of bed or border, or an otherwise useless narrow strip by fence or wall. Full sun is needed for the first sowings in March/April but later ones will tolerate partial shade.

Under cloches the first sowing may be made in February. Room may sometimes be found beside another crop, but if radishes only are to occupy the cloches they should be sown broadcast to make full use of the space. Get a fine tilth, mark out the area to be cloched, and move about 1 in. of the top soil to the sides. Sprinkle the seed evenly over this very shallow depression and rake the soil back over it. This gives a much more even plant than the traditional method of broadcasting the seed on the surface and raking it in. Remember that in bright windy weather in March cloches dry out quickly and water may be needed. Don't wait for the roots to reach 'market size', eat them small and tender and sow more. If you let any of them go to seed you can try the seed-pods, sliced, in salads and even, it is said, in sandwiches.

Varieties. French Breakfast, Sparkler, and Red Forcing are all suitable for early crops. Scarlet Globe and Inca for summer sowings, the latter a new variety retaining its eating qualities even when allowed to grow large. To ensure a succession several varieties may be mixed and sown together, but if this means buying more seed than you really want a selected mixture is obtainable from Suttons for only 4p a packet. The winter varieties China Rose and Black Spanish are sown in July and lifted and stored in damp sand. They grow very large and when peeled and sliced for salads are crisp and mild-flavoured.

SPRING ONIONS

Salad onions are sown March/April in wide drills, rather more thickly than radishes and about 1 in. deep. They may need careful hand weeding in the early stages, being fragile and easily smothered by weeds. The variety used is White Lisbon.

Where space is very limited spring onions are not the best onion-flavoured salad. A more continuous supply is obtained from chives, listed among the herbs in Chapter 6. No garden should be without a few clumps of chives, for they grow in any soil, in sun or shade, and can be increased by division of the clumps at almost any time of year. One important point—chives should be cut down when the flowers appear in summer and kept well watered to encourage a fresh growth of young 'grass'.

The Welsh Onion is another useful perennial member of the family. The origin of its name is obscure, since it came from Siberia and is therefore extremely hardy. Its general appearance is that of a tightly-packed bunch of spring onions which multiply during the growing season. The tops remain perennially green even during severe winter weather and below ground there is a white stem but no bulb.

Welsh onions should be divided every other year in spring if you want plenty of new young stems. They will grow in any soil but prefer a well-drained one.

Plants of the Welsh onion are obtainable from suppliers of

97

herbs (Laxton & Bunyard, for instance). They may also be grown from seed sown in shallow drills in April and thinned to 6 in.

TOMATOES

The best tomato is one fully ripened on the vine, and this is one good reason for growing your own. Another is that you can try varieties of high quality which the commercial grower, because of convention and market pressures, will never produce for you. Here we are concerned with outdoor and cloche growing. Greenhouse culture is dealt with in Chapter 5.

Soil and Cultivation. The tomato will grow and fruit in most soils, but a cold, wet, heavy one gives it less chance of cropping well in the open air than the lighter and warmer types. Compost, bonfire ashes, and a few handfuls of peat can be forked in before planting; a soil too rich in nitrogen encourages luxuriant growth and this is no help, especially in dwarf varieties under cloches.

Plant in a sheltered position in late May or early June, choosing if possible a spot that will catch the sun in September, when the days are shorter and the fruit is ripening. Space 18 in. apart, and if the plants are a bit 'leggy' it will do no harm to plant rather deeply, burying an inch or so of bare stem. Tall varieties must have a good stake and adequate tying. Watering should aim at keeping the soil consistently moist in dry spells—alternate drying-out and heavy soaking causes the fruit to split.

Growing under Cloches. Dwarf varieties are planted 2 ft. distance, one to each growers barn cloche. Mid-May is early enough, nothing is gained by planting before reasonable night temperatures are assured—tomatoes which get chilled turn an unhealthy blue and sulk for weeks.

There are three main problems associated with cloched tomatoes: keeping the ripening fruit from contact with the ground, suppressing weeds which get entangled with the prostrate growth, and a steady supply of moisture. The answer to all three is a mulch of black polythene. A strip rather wider than the cloches is laid down along the length of the site, holes are cut in it at 2 ft. intervals and the toms. planted through them. The row is kept weed-free, the fruit clean and safe from slugs, the black surface absorbs daytime heat and radiates it at night, and soil moisture is retained. When watering is neccessary the side of each cloche can be slightly raised and the hose-end or watering-can spout inserted *under* the polythene.

An initial watering is given after planting and the cloches kept tightly closed up for a week or two, after which they should be spaced $\frac{1}{2}$ in. apart for ventilation. Some thinning out of unwanted shoots and branches may be needed and the plants should not be allowed to carry more than four or five trusses of fruit.

Growing Outdoors in Containers. Tomatoes in pots or boxes are good subjects for a sunny courtyard and some varieties are practicable in a window-box. A 10 or 12 in. flower-pot, a wooden box or even a galvanized or plastic bucket with a hole in it, will accomodate the tall-growing varieties. But this is dealt with more fully in Chapter 6.

Training and Stopping. Except for the bush or dwarf sorts, tomatoes are grown as a single stem. The side-shoots which appear at the base and in the leaf axils are rubbed out as soon as noticed, and early in August the growing point is removed to prevent any more fruit setting. Don't delay this until later in the hope of a bigger crop, even in the south of England. After this stopping there may be a fresh outburst of side shoots from the base and even from the tips of the fruit trusses; these will retard ripening if not removed. Keep your mind on the job when rubbing out side-shoots or you may find that you have mistakenly obliterated a bloom truss which cannot be replaced.

Buying Plants. They are on sale in every garden shop and chain store, usually appearing much too early for safe planting outdoors. One is sometimes told to select plants showing the first truss of bloom, but the more important criteria are stocky, short-jointed growth, a bright green colour, and, perhaps, the seed-leaves showing near the base of the plant. These are indications that the tomato has been grown without a check and has the vigour to carry on.

Hints on growing from seed are given in Chapter 5.

Varieties. Tall-growing types for the open air: Outdoor Girl, Essex Wonder, Moneymaker, Open Air (Thompson & Morgan). Large Continental type fruit: Marmande (Sutton). Yellow varieties: Golden Queen and Dobies' Peach.

Bush varieties for cloches: Amateur Improved, Bush

Lebanon, Sleaford Abundance. The last is a new introduction, said to crop well and ripen its fruit in bad summers.

Pests and Diseases. No pests except slugs when fruit is allowed to rest on the ground. Potato Blight is the one really serious disease, rotting the fruit before it has a chance to ripen. It is widespread only in wet seasons and appears to be worst in rural areas, where infection spreads from potato crops. Spray with Bordeaux Mixture if you hear reports of the disease on potatoes.

CHAPTER FIVE

Greenhouse Crops

BUYING A GREENHOUSE

REPAIRS AND EQUIPMENT

AUBERGINES

CUCUMBERS

FORCED RHUBARB AND CHICORY

THE GRAPE VINE

LETTUCE

MELONS

STRAWBERRIES

SWEET PEPPERS

TOMATOES

Greenhouse Crops

It may be asked if a greenhouse has a place in the small garden where space is at a premium. What does one get out of it that can justify giving it standing room?

The short answer is that a space enclosed in glass is far more valuable horticulturally than the same space in the open. It will produce a greater weight of tomatoes, cucumbers, melons, grapes and other tender things than can possibly be grown on an equivalent area in the open or even under cloches or frames. It makes the raising of plants for subsequent planting out a more certain process than the use of the kitchen window-sill, where there is often too much warmth and not enough light. It means that you can carry on gardening when the weather drives you indoors.

Most gardeners who have no greenhouse would like one. More's the pity, then, that anyone lucky enough to possess this valuable asset should allow it to fall into disrepair, or be used as a repository for junk and moribund plants.

BUYING A GREENHOUSE

Size and cost may be determined by the available site and by the depth of your pocket, but even within such limits there is a wide choice. Make no decision until you have thumbed through a good pile of catalogues.

The cheapest house to buy is the conventional softwood type, the next cheapest is the western red cedar or African hardwood, and the dearest the aluminium framed. Maintenance costs are in reverse order; an aluminium house never needs painting, a cedarwood one requires an occasional treatment with a special preservative, but deal or softwood must be painted regularly or trouble is certain. As one who heartily detests painting glass structures I would always plump for cedar, even if it meant a size smaller than I could afford in deal. These unpainted houses have an appearance and 'feel' of warmth which aluminium lacks.

Design is a matter for personal preference and the kind of things you intend to grow. If you want to plant direct in the ground the house must be glazed to ground-level to ensure adequate light. Where all growing is in containers staging is neccessary and the sides can be of timber or metal up to 3 ft. The best of both worlds is obtained by having glass to the ground and removable staging—which you can make quite cheaply to suit your own ideas.

Reasonable height to the eaves is important and so is a decently wide doorway. The house should be sited to catch maximum sunlight, especially in winter. In a small garden it will have to be near the dwelling house, and this is all to the good. A greenhouse always in full view is usually better to look at, and its occupants better attended, than one tucked away out of sight. There is a lot to be said for a lean-to conservatory type structure against the house, it is convenient to work and relatively cheap to heat. The Victorians made good use of their conservatories, and in a truly civilized community a conservatory should be a standard adjunct like a garage. Consult your local planning authority before erecting a conservatory or indeed any other type of greenhouse.

As far as constructional details are concerned, puttyless glazing is preferable in a house erected without professional help. And I would also opt for a manufacturer who supplies ready-made foundations in the form of interlocking concrete sleepers.

REPAIRS AND EQUIPMENT

A dilapidated greenhouse can usually be repaired by an average D.I.Y. enthusiast for much less than the cost of a new one, provided the main framing is still sound. The roof glazing bars are the most vulnerable point after the actual glass, but often one or two need replacement while the majority have some years of useful life. Where there is evidence of drip through the roof this can be checked and the bars preserved by using Sylglas foil-backed sealing tape. This useful product is basically aluminium foil with a strongly adhesive surface and wide enough to go right over the glazing bar and stick to the glass on either side. Applied when glass and woodwork are perfectly dry (a hot summer's day is best for the job) it can save you the tedious work of removing the glass and re-puttying. I have some on an old house at the moment which has survived three winters and is still bright and waterproof.

Heating. The maintenance of high temperatures is unnecessary and too expensive, but a small house is much more useful if you can keep frost out in winter and provide a little artificial warmth in early spring for raising tender subjects like tomatoes, cucumbers, and peppers.

The choice of fuel lies between electricity and paraffin. Oil heaters are the cheaper to run in terms of costs per unit, but need more attention and may not be cheaper overall because they are not thermostatically controlled. All heating appliance manufacturers give the output of their heaters in British Thermal Units (BTUs), and there is a simple formula for reckoning the output needed to keep out frost: Surface area of structure in sq. ft. × 20 = BTUs per hour needed to maintain 35°F when the outside temperature is 20°F. Thus a house 8 by 6 ft., span roofed and 6 ft. to the eaves, has a surface area of very roughly 250 sq. ft. Multiplied by 20, this gives a requirement of 5,000 BTUs per hour to keep he temperature inside at 35°F. when it falls to 20°F. or 12 degrees of frost outside. The guide is only a rough one and temperatures do sometimes fall below 20 degrees, though only rarely in large towns. But it is worth measuring up your greenhouse and keeping the resultant sum in mind when buying a heater. For instance, an Aladdin heater with a 2 in. burner puts out 5,580 BTUs and a 2kw. electric fan heater 6,800 BTUs, so the 8 by 6 ft. house would be safe with either, but a 10 by 8 ft. one might not.

The thermostat is an essential part of any type of electrical heating, switching it on and off as the temperature varies—and it can vary with sun heat more than is often realized. A sunny February afternoon may push it up into the 70s and obviously no artificial warmth is then needed until it falls to about 40°F. after sundown. A paraffin heater may be kept continuously burning where an electrical one is only actually operative for a fraction of the twenty-four hours. Moreover, electricity consumption is greatest at night, so if your installation is on a white meter you can benefit from off-peak rates.

Do not use a domestic fan-heater—only one designed for the job. Choose a make with a built-in thermostat, this correctly monitors the air temperature and will not give a false reading as sometimes happens with a wrongly sited thermostat. All electrical work in a greenhouse is best done by a professional, conditions are usually damp and any fault in earthing or insulation is dangerous.

Minor Equipment and Materials. Pots and seed trays are essential but should be bought only as required. Polystyrene pots are available everywhere and seem to suit most plants just as well as the heavier and more fragile clays. The main difference is that no moisture is lost by absorption so that plants in plastic pots must not be over-watered. Peat pots (Jiffy-pots) are admirable for raising anything to be transplanted, but of course have to be bought afresh as plant and pot go into the ground together. Rings or 'Tompots' for the ring culture of tomatoes can be bought in cardboard for one season's use, or in polystyrene to last indefinitely.

The use of proper composts for seed-sowing and growing-on is vital. The John Innes may be bought at any seed shop, but vary in quality. This is because a basic ingredient of the JI range is sterilized loam, and if a poor quality loam is used the compost is affected even though the JI formula is adhered to. So JI composts should come from a first class supplier and as they deteriorate slightly in stock too much should not be bought at one time. If you can obtain decent topsoil from any source you can make up your own unsterilized JI potting compost. The formula is: 7 parts loose bulk of loam; 3 parts of peat; 2 parts of coarse sand; 4 oz. JI Base per bushel of mixture. Mix the loam and peat, then mix the JI Base (bought from the garden shop) into the sand. Thoroughly mix all together. A bushel is the amount contained by a box measuring 22 by 10 by 10 in.

Although unsterilized compost is perfectly satisfactory for the larger plants it is better to use the purchased JI or a soil-less compost for seed-sowing to avoid the risk of damping off.

A useful piece of greenhouse equipment is a propagator. This is simply a glass-topped case in which seeds can be germinated and cuttings rooted at a somewhat higher temperature than in the rest of the house. It may be bought in various elaborate forms, but four lengths of straight-edged board, butt-jointed to form a square frame, covered with sheets of glass and standing on a solid base covered with peat or gravel, will cost little. The extra warmth can come from a paraffin heater under the frame, or from a length of soil-heating cable embedded in the peat or other material. This is the ideal method of providing gentle warmth; enough cable for 10 sq. ft. of frame has a loading of only 75 watts and is negligible in running costs and completely safe.

AUBERGINES

The aubergine or egg-plant is a native of the tropics and not worth attempting in the open air. Those who enjoy its rather sinister-looking fruit may well give it a place in the greenhouse, thought it requires a lot of space in relation to the actual crop.

Sowing. Delay this until you can maintain a day temperature of 60°F. in dull weather and of at least 50°F. at night. If you have a propagator this may be achieved as early as March, but if the house is normally heated only enough to keep out frost it never pays to be impatient. Severe night frosts can occur in March and even April and indoor temperatures fall low enough to check the more tender things. This applies specifically to aubergines, peppers, cucumbers, melons and tomatoes. In most seasons the amateur with only modest heating equipment is well advised to leave the seeds of all these in their packets until the outdoor daffodils are past their best.

Sowing of all the smaller seeds under glass is done in the same way. When it is intended to sow in a seed tray or box this is filled with compost to within ½ in. of the top. The compost is made level and firm and is watered if at all dry; this pre-sowing watering is important in dampening the compost all through and in avoiding overhead watering immediately after sowing, which if done carelessly can leave the seeds uncovered or washed into heaps. Sprinkle the seed thinly and evenly, cover with only enough compost to prevent any of it being visible, and either cover the tray or place it in the propagator. The old advice to cover with a sheet of glass and brown paper is very sound; you want to reduce evaporation and prevent direct sunlight falling on the surface and drying it out. The close atmosphere of the propagator does this even better, but even there you must inspect the seed trays daily and water through a fine rose.

Pricking out is the operation of moving seedlings to other

trays or pots where they will have room to develop. The earlier this is done the better, it has been shown that tomatoes pricked out in the seed-leaf stage have a lifelong advantage over those whose first move is left until their true leaves have begun to appear. Lift the seedling carefully with a plant label or penknife, always holding the little plant by a seed-leaf and never by the stem, and firm it gently into a hole made in the potting compost. Where the sowing has been direct into peat pots it is only neccessary to pull out all but one seedling and leave that one to grow on undisturbed.

Returning from the general to aubergines in particular, it must be said that they are slow to germinate, even in moderate warmth. Give them three weeks before starting to get worried. It must also be said that aubergines, like peppers only more so, don't take kindly to being moved and are better sown in peat pots and put straight into fruiting quarters when these become full of roots.

Planted directly in the ground in a greenhouse border they should be 15 in. apart. A 7 or 8 in. pot is big enough if a good potting compost is used. Leave a 2 in. space at the top for the addition of more compost when fruiting begins. Occasional liquid manure feeds are helpful, but must be stopped before the fruit is full-grown or it may split. Plants are best kept close to the glass to prevent them becoming 'leggy', and they benefit from syringing and a moist atmosphere.

The plants must be restricted to four fruits apiece. At a height of 15 in. nip out the growing point and allow two laterals to develop. When four fruits have definitely set the laterals are themselves stopped and any more side-shoots removed. The variety usually grown is Long Purple. Fruit should be picked in September from an April sowing.

CUCUMBERS

Indoor cucumbers need an organically-rich soil, plenty of water but good drainage, and generally warm and moist surroundings. They have no great love of fresh air, preferring a steamy fug, and this makes them awkward companions for other greenhouse crops. However, the variety Conqueror does quite well under conditions that suit tomatoes and the outdoor hybrids mentioned in Chapter 4 will all thrive with the extra protection of a greenhouse. But all cucumbers may need shading at times.

Sowing. Don't attempt it until late April, even if the house is heated or a propagator is available. A temperature of around 70°F. is required for germination, and the quicker this takes place the stronger the plant. Sow two or three seeds to a 3 in. or peat pot, using JI or proprietary potting compost, not more than $\frac{1}{2}$ in. deep. Reduce to one on germination.

Planting Out. A slightly raised bed on the greenhouse floor or large containers on the staging will do equally well. Even 12 in. pots are not really big enough, wooden boxes about 10 in. deep and a foot wide and any convenient length, are better. Use a mixture of soil, garden compost, peat, or any bulky organic material you can get hold of. Form it into a low ridge shape and set the cucumbers along the apex. They should be 2 ft. apart whether in a continuous bed or separate boxes, and be planted when they have not more than four adult leaves.

Training and Pollination. Apart from regular watering and damping down of path and woodwork in warm weather, the main attention needed is the tying up of stem and laterals. Horizontal wires about 9 in. apart are a useful form of support, the vine being tied to each wire as it grows up, and the laterals always having wires handy to which they too may be tied. A full-grown cucumber is pretty weighty, and the laterals on which the fruit is borne must be supported as soon as it begins to swell. Stop each lateral two leaves beyond a growing fruit, and stop the main vine when it reaches its allotted height. More side-shoots will be formed to continue cropping, but a cucumber usually fruits in 'flushes'. By about August it may look finished, but a top-dressing of compost and continued attention to watering will stimulate a further— if rather badly shaped—crop.

The question of pollination must be understood in relation to three different types:

(1) The indoor cucumbers like Conqueror and Telegraph grow without fertilization. If fertilized they form seeds and become 'bull-nosed' and bitter. Pick off all the male blooms and if possible keep the house shut against pollinating insects such as bees. The male blooms are distinguishable by their having no baby cucumber at the base of the flower.

(2) The second group is that of the new all-female hybrids.

The best known varieties are Femina and Fertila. There are practically no male flowers to worry about, but so many female ones are produced that they must be thinned to reduce the load on the plant. The fruit develop unfertilized and are of as good a quality as any grown. Follow directions of the suppliers.

(3) The outdoor climbing varieties, Kaga, Kyoto, and Baton Vert. These would be easy to grow with the protection of even a cold house, but the female flowers *must* be fertilized. If the fruit fail to swell, transfer pollen directly as advised for marrows.

FORCED RHUBARB AND CHICORY

If heating is maintained through the winter, the space under the staging should not be wasted. Rhubarb lifted and grown there is ready a month before the covered outdoor product, and boxes of chicory roots may be blanched in succession.

Rhubarb. Crowns for forcing are lifted early in December and left lying exposed on the ground for a week or so. Exposure to harsh conditions induces the buds to awaken more quickly from dormancy when brought into warmth. In the event of very dry, freezing winds, though, the roots should be brought in immediately. They should be dug up carefully to avoid damage to the very fleshy roots.

Warmth, moisture, and complete darkness are needed for success. The crowns are embedded in moist peat or compost, and enclosed in a dark space where the stems have plenty of room to grow. A deep box or tea chest covered with black polythene is one possible arrangement, but there may be others better suited to your own greenhouse.

Chicory blanching is described in the previous chapter. The warm greenhouse is a good place for it, but the boxes of roots must have a completely light-tight covering. Anything grown under staging must also be protected from drip, which is the worst sort of uncontrolled watering.

THE GRAPE VINE

In the singular, of course. One vine is as much as the small-greenhouse owner will have room for, and if he fails to discipline it properly he will soon find there is not even room for himself. A properly trained and pruned vine is not only more fruitful but allows the greenhouse to be used for other purposes. The grape is of course *the* under-glass fruit, and however well it does in the open will always do better with protection.

Planting. The general advice given in Chapter 2 is applicable, good drainage, a not very rich soil, and careful planting with the roots well spread out. But first you must decide whether to plant inside the greenhouse or just outside with the vine coming through a hole in the wall. This is the best arrangement for the amateur without much heat at his disposal because the vine is less likely to start into growth too early if its roots are in the colder soil outside. It must be planted as close as possible to the end wall of the greenhouse and in hard frost the exposed stem should be wrapped in sacking.

Cut back to two or three buds after planting and keep only one growth, the strongest, to be passed into the greenhouse and form the main stem. It is taken up to the roof and trained along it, being allowed to lengthen each season until it reaches the far end. This stem and its fruiting laterals are eventually tied to wires attached to the roof timbers, but young vine growth is very brittle and must be tied into place as gently as possible. It should be suspended well below the roof so that the foliage is not in contact with the glass where it might be sun-scorched. Pruning is basically the same as for outdoor vines, laterals being pinched back in the summer to six leaves where no fruit is carried or to two leaves beyond a fruit bunch. All should be cut back to two or three buds when the vine is dormant in winter.

The flower clusters will probably appear in May—it depends rather upon the temperature at which the house has been kept—and the blossom usually sets well if the house is freely ventilated on hot days and a 'growing' atmosphere is maintained by damping down and occasionally spraying.

If you have time it pays to thin the bunches when the berries are a bit bigger than sweet pea seed. On a good bunch about two-thirds of the fruit should be cut out, leaving the remainder evenly spaced. Not only does this mean finer grapes but less danger of mould through the berries being packed closely together. Grape scissors—long pointed things —are the tool for the job; the bunch should not be held with the fingers but steadied with a forked stick about 9 in. long as the berries are snipped out. Ideally, they should be left ½ in. apart.

Varieties. Black Hamburgh (the Hampton Court vine) is the beginner's best bet, with Buckland Sweetwater for a white.

LETTUCE

Winter lettuce is a useful greenhouse crop if it can be finished up before all the space is needed for spring and summer sowings. A worthwhile quantity can be produced from a completely unheated house when sown in borders. In fact, for a small glass-to-ground house with no heating the two most profitable crops are probably winter lettuce followed by ring culture tomatoes.

Sowing and Cultivation. In the cold house the procedure is the same as under cloches (Chapter 4). The house is really a very large cloche, but being that much larger the body of air it contains cools more slowly than under cloches after being warmed by the sun. This means a slightly higher average winter temperature and hearted lettuce in April instead of May.

Sow in October, in drills 9 in. apart in the borders if they are free. Thin by stages to 9 in. apart in the rows; some of the later thinnings may be of usable size. If the borders are still occupied by tomatoes, don't delay sowing. Sow in a seed tray, prick out into boxes of potting compost, and plant out in the borders when the latter are free—any time up to the end of November.

Soil should be enriched by digging in garden compost and a light dressing of a nitrogenous organic such as dried blood. Keep the soil consistently moist, but water carefully between the plants and avoid splashing the leaves. Open the ventilators on bright days for a few hours around mid-day, but keep them closed during cold, damp, foggy periods. Remove any lower leaves which show signs of decay.

Varieties. May Queen, Sutton's Premier, or Unrivalled. A number of new Dutch varieties (obtainable from most seedsmen) are coming into use. 'Kwiek' matures in early winter in a cold house if sown by mid-August, and 'Kloek' is ready by early April from an October sowing. 'Kloek' is also suitable for a slightly warmed house, in which it can be fully hearted by March.

MELONS

They need the same treatment as cucumbers, but there are a few differences to be noted.

The melon plant needs full exposure to sun and should never be shaded. Soil is best made not too rich, fine bone meal is a useful additive, but a liquid manure given when the fruit is swelling is the safest feed. Plants are set 3 ft. apart and always on a mound or ridge to prevent stem rot. Reduce watering to a minimum when the fruit begins to ripen.

All melons must be fertilized; strip the corolla from the male bloom, press the stamens into the female flower, and leave there. Try to fertilize three or four blooms simultaneously because if one fruit gets too far ahead of the others it swells at their expense and checks their development. Not more than four per plant should be permitted.

The general training of main stem and laterals is the same as for cucumbers, but once four fruits have set any new side-shoots must be pinched back. Fruit-bearing laterals must be carefully tied, and large individual fruits may have to be supported in melon nets.

Varieties. The old favourite Hero of Lockinge, and Sutton's King George are true 'house' melons which the amateur could attempt with confidence. The hardier Cantaloupe Charantais, the small melon so popular in France, could be sown in May in a cold house and fruit August/September. So could the new pink fleshed hybrid Sweetie.

STRAWBERRIES

Early strawberries grown in pots are among the more interesting luxuries. If you have a strawberry bed in the garden producing surplus runners they need cost you nothing but a little time and trouble.

Raising the Pot Plants. Strawberries to fruit in May must be established in their pots the previous August. For this you need early rooted runners and the traditional advice is to root them direct into small pots to minimize disturbance later. The method is to sink 3 in. pots filled with compost into the ground beside the strawberry row and peg down a runner into each pot. The pots have to be regularly watered if the runner is to root and the young plant develop.

The disadvantage of this method is if you forget to water the pots for a few days in dry weather the young plants may die; the compost, especially in plastic pots, may dry out completely while the surrounding soil is relatively moist. For this reason I prefer to let runners root naturally in the ground.

Keep an eye on the first runners to appear and try to get them rooted as early as possible. Loosen the soil under the runner at the point where the cadet plant is beginning to grow and hold it down with a stone or a piece of bent wire. Keep the surface moist and nip off any extension of the runner if it starts to grow again after the young plant is rooted.

Potting and Wintering. If you start pegging down runners in late June they should be well rooted by mid-August. They are then established in 5 or 6 in. pots, using JI. Potting No. 3 or a home-made equivalent. They would probably do well in Levington, Bowers or other soil-less compost, but my own experience is limited to growing in soil.

The rooted runners should be thoroughly soaked before lifting, which is done carefully with a trowel, keeping all the roots and the soil round them intact. Plant one runner per pot, not in the centre but slightly towards one side, so that the ripening fruit may be induced to hang over the edge.

The pots are stood close together in a slightly shady place outdoors, and watered daily in dry weather. Care at this stage is essential as the plants are already building up the next year's fruiting potential. In October they are ready to become dormant for a few months and the pots may be transferred to a cold frame or sunk to the rims in the ground to prevent the roots freezing. If the greenhouse is absolutely unheated—if you leave it cold until seed sowing starts in spring,—the strawberries may spend the winter in it. They must not be brought into artificial warmth until they have had a rest at winter temperatures.

Once growth starts a night temperature of 45°F. is about right, rising as high in the daytime as sun heat will take it. The plants should be in flower by the end of March or beginning of April and on sunny days the greenhouse ventilators should be opened to admit any pollinating insects that may be about.

The strawberries' maximum demand for water is when the fruit is swelling and liquid manure should also be given at this stage. When the berries begin to ripen they should not be splashed and the trusses should be directed over the pot rim or propped up with forked twigs.

Varieties. Cambridge Favourite or Royal Sovereign, but the latter only if you have good virus-free stock. Cambridge Vigour and Merton Herald crop rather earlier than the other two.

If unable to produce your own plants you may order pot-grown runners from one of the suppliers in our list. Ask for August delivery and place the order in spring or early summer.

Perpetual varieties are useless for early fruit, but runners of Sans Rivale, rooted in summer and potted up, may be brought in for fruitng in October.

Raising Alpine Strawberries from Seed. A single packet of seed will provide scores of plants, and if you can make an early start you will pick fruit in the same year.

In a warm greenhouse, sow in February; in a completely cold one, wait until April. Sow in seed compost, thinly, in tray or shallow box. Cover with glass and paper, keep moist, and don't be impatient. Strawberries germinate very erratically and the appearance of a few seedlings in advance of the majority may deceive you into blaming the seed. Ultimately, germination is always very good.

Prick out into deeper trays of potting compost, 2 in. apart, or into small pots, when big enough to handle. Growth is rapid from this point and the plants will soon be big enough to go out in the garden. February sowings will begin to fruit in July and the later ones will produce a few berries in the autumn. All will be large fruiting plants by the following year.

Varieties. Baron Solemacher is stocked by all seedsmen. Dobies' Delicious and another new variety, Alexandria (Thompson & Morgan) are probably larger fruited. Another kind easily raised from seed is described by its name—Alpine Yellow. Reports give it full marks for quality.

SWEET PEPPERS

Better known by this name than by their botanical one of capsicum, although it is under the latter that you are most likely to find them in the seedman's catalogue. Green and red peppers are not two different varieties, the red is a fully ripened green one, and does not usually attain this colour until some time after picking. From the culinary point of view the fruit is best used green.

Sowing and Cultivation. Same as for aubergines, but the pepper is a hardier plant and tolerant of slightly lower temperatures in its early life. Even so it should not be sown until late April in a cold house or a month earlier where some warmth or a propagator is available. About 60°F. is needed to start the seed. Sow in Jiffy-pots or thumb pots, three or four seeds to each, reduce to one seedling, and plant in permanent quarters before the pots are overcrowded with roots.

J.I. No. 3 or a soil-less potting compost are suitable, and a rather smaller container than for tomato growing can be used; a 7 or 8 in. pot is big enough. Leave 2 in. at the top for the addition of extra compost when the plant begins to fruit. A weekly feed of liquid manure may also be given then, but is less important than it is to aubergines. The pepper grows about 2 ft. high and when in fruit may need supporting with thin canes. Fruiting need not be restricted as with the aubergine.

Peppers may be grown under cloches and for this purpose should be raised in the greenhouse and planted out in late May.

Varieties. Not much choice. The short form known as Bull-nosed Red is the typical one for greenhouse culture, and Dobies' Outdoor Pepper is a new one for choice growing. The Hot or Cayenne Pepper is usually listed as Chili and is grown in the same way as sweet varieties.

TOMATOES

Perhaps the most popular greenhouse crop. Tomatoes may be grown from seed or bought as plants. They will grow in a heated house or in one with no artificial heat. They can be planted in the greenhouse border or in containers.

Sowing. Sow in March if some warmth is available. A propagator is useful. In a cold house it may be better to buy plants in April rather than try to raise your own.

Sow as described under Aubergines, using sterilized or soil-less compost. Prick out the seedlings into small pots the moment they are big enough to handle. Maintain as good a night temperature as possible, and keep the plants close to the glass to induce sturdy growth.

Plants being raised for outdoor growing, especially the quick-growing bush varieties, should not be sown until early

April, otherwise they become pot-bound and starved before it is safe to plant them out.

Growing Methods. Plants may be set out 18 in. apart in the greenhouse border and in new ground will yield good crops with a minimum of attention. In particular, they are much less likely to suffer from lack of water in hot weather than are those in pots. There is, however, a danger of disease if they are grown there year after year, and the border will have to be rested or the soil in it replaced.

The method known as ring culture may be used either at ground level or on the staging; in the former case it enables you to grow tomatoes *on* the border but not actually in the soil, obviating the risk of disease. The tomato is planted in a bottomless pot or 'ring' made of plastic or cardboard and filled with JI Potting No. 3. The ring stands on a bed of 'aggregate', a 5 in. deep layer of some material which holds water but has itself no feeding value. Heavy aggregates like sand or pulverized clinker are still sometimes recommended, but one might just as well use a lighter substance. Peat is cheapest and quite good; so is vermiculite, and so is a new material developed specifically for this sort of job, Lytag 6M. The aggregate bed is built up on the border, or on tin sheeting on the staging. The open-ended pots are stood on it and filled with compost, and the tomatoes planted. Masses of root penetrate the aggregate which is kept well watered, so that the plant has a consistent water supply. Liquid feeds are applied to the compost in the rings.

Tomatoes in ordinary containers need at least a 10 in. pot of good compost, and a weekly liquid feed once the first truss has set. Watering is a problem if one has to be away all day—one of the advantages of ring culture—but in very hot weather the ventilators should be left wide and the door partly open, so that the temperature is at least kept below the hundred mark.

The plants must be trained as single stems up wires, strings or stakes. Tying is time-consuming and the quickest supporting method is soft twine from the roof to a peg in the ground near each plant. Tomato stem and twine are twisted spirally round one another as the plant grows. All side shoots are rubbed out and the tomato stopped when it can go no further or the season is getting too late for ripening. The practicable number of trusses varies, but it will be greater than with open-air plants. The new variety Infinity Cross is usually stopped after the fourth truss.

A moist, growing atmosphere helps the flowers to set, and from the time the first truss blooms overhead spraying also assists setting. This is best done in the heat of the day, so that the plants don't go to bed with leaves and fruit wet.

Varieties. Moneymaker and Ailsa Craig are reliable conventional choices. If you want a large Continental type you cannot beat Big Boy; I've grown this many times and although the first truss is difficult to set the final yield of heavy, solid fruit is usually as good as its flavour. Infinity Cross (Thompson and Morgan) is a new break. It has large, spreading trusses each bearing up to 4 lb. of medium-sized fruit of high quality. Obviously, with trusses of this size, the number carried per plant must be rather more limited than in most varieties.

Among yellow tomatoes Dobies' Peach is as easy to grow as any red sort, attractive in appearance and of non-acid flavour. Those wanting something really way-out could try White (Thompson and Morgan), an American introduction of the palest yellow tint. Quality and cropping are said to be excellent—but of course the Americans also have a preference for white eggs.

CHAPTER SIX

Crops in and around the House

WINDOW-BOXES AND OTHER
   CONTAINERS
BEAN SPROUTS
FRUIT TREES IN POTS AND TUBS
HERBS
MUSHROOMS
MUSTARD AND CRESS
SALADS IN CONTAINERS
THE STRAWBERRY BARREL
WINDOW-BOX STRAWBERRIES

Crops in and around the House

We have been thinking about gardens, plots of real soil and spaces big enough for greenhouses. But what if you have no garden, or only a strip of the good earth so minute that not even an estate agent could magnify it into a desirable feature? Restricting, of course, but not fatal.

You have a yard, courtyard, patio, terrace, or whatever your neighbourhood insists on calling it. You have a house, balcony, window-sill, garage, shed, or cellar. You can afford to buy or make containers of some sort and to fill them with a proprietary compost in which anything will grow. The range of possible subjects is greater than we have space to catalogue here and there's plenty of room for experiment. Look at the variety which the window-box and tub enthusiasts have brought into the decorative side of container-growing.

WINDOW-BOXES AND OTHER CONTAINERS

A window-box must be properly constructed and installed. Other containers—pots, tubs, and troughs—will no doubt stand entirely within your own territory, but a window-box may be of concern to other people. A shower of muddy water is maybe forgivable, but a direct hit by a receptacle containing a half-hundredweight of compost is something else again.

Fortunately, any such tragedy is unneccessary with modern boxes and fittings, and even a D.I.Y. wooden job can be securely fastened and equipped with the shallow drip-tray made for the purpose.

The length of a box is determined by that of the window ledge; if you want to be able to lift it in and out easily leave a 2 in. clearance of the window frame at either end. The ideal depth is 9 in. and width 10 in., but purchased boxes are usually a little smaller. Home-made boxes are generally in softwood and the interior must then be well treated with Cuprinol. Drainage holes of $\frac{1}{2}$ in. diameter should be spaced 6 in. apart diagonally from corner to corner.

Many types of wooden box are on the market and of these the luxury choice is of course teak. Fibreglass is also fairly expensive and almost everlasting, but the many plastic makes with a simulated stone finish are relatively cheap, quite nice to look at, and above all beautifully light to handle.

Other adjuncts of container-growing, tubs, troughs, pots, plant stands, hanging baskets and all, proliferate in every garden shop and catalogue. It's a matter of making the sensible choice for the things you intend to grow. Tubs and the largest pots for fruit trees, smaller sizes of pot for tomatoes, and the long ornamental troughs for herbs, all are available in both heavy timber and light plastic. Mushroom trays are usually home-made or adapted from shallow wooden boxes.

Around-the-house gardening requires very little equipment. A trowel, hand fork, and a four-pint watering can with a long spout and detachable rose and you are ready. A household bucket is quickest for watering the large items like fruits trees, and for them you will also eventually need a pair of secateurs.

One overall warning about container-growing in the open: never assume that a plant in a pot, be it a tree or a tomato, has been adequately watered by rainfall. Even an inch of rain may fail to reach the crowded roots near the bottom of the container.

BEAN SPROUTS

This standard ingredient of Chinese cookery is easily grown. Fresh sprouts are better than canned ones and far better than the poor little dried things.

The Chinese emperor who is supposed to have written in praise of bean sprouts in the year 2939 B.C. probably discovered, like the first maltsters, that a lot of changes take place when a seed germinates. For one thing, there is a vast increase in vitamin content. Sprouted wheat contains 30 per cent more B1 and 200 per cent more B2 than the dormant grain, and all seeds show similar changes. In America it is now possible to buy elaborate home sprouters, and not only every sort of bean but even alfalfa and watercress seed is being added to the menu.

Mung and soy are the two most usual varieties for sprouting. Mung beans are obtainable from Suttons but you may have to shop around for soy. The beans are soaked in water at room temperature for forty-eight hours and then placed on damp flannel or Kleenex tissues in a plastic tray. Spread them in a close layer but not piled up. Keep in a warm dark place, such as the airing cupboard, and never allow them to dry out. To help in this the tray may be enclosed in a polythene bag, but this should be removed when the sprouts are in actual contact with it. They are ready in about a week and are used when 2 in. long and nice and plump.

FRUIT TREES IN POTS AND TUBS

The practice of growing fully mature fruiting trees in containers is over a hundred years old. The original idea was to make it possible to bring them into the greenhouse and obtain early fruit. The Victorians were also delighted to have fruit-laden trees borne into the dining-room for the admiration and sustenance of guests.

Pioneers in this field were the nurserymen Thomas Rivers and Sons, who by the 1890s already had trees which had been growing in pots for twenty-five years, and who are still the acknowledged experts. Talking to Messrs. Rivers just before writing this confirmed me in thinking that if you have no greenhouse or garden but only a courtyard, balcony or roof garden you can still grow a variety of fruit.

Essential requirements for success are:

The trees must be fully exposed to light during the growing season. This does not mean full sun all day long, merely that they must not be shadowed by an overhanging roof.

In summer, and especially when bearing fruit, the trees must be watered at least once a day, perhaps more often according to conditions. This has to be done as religiously as feeding a pet.

When dormant, say from October to March, the soil in the pots must still be kept damp and must not be allowed to freeze solid; this would damage the roots and perhaps split the pots. The trees could be wintered in an unheated shed or garage, but *not* in a centrally heated house. If brought into warmth without full light the leaf and fruit buds would develop prematurely and come to nothing. At Rivers' nurseries the pots are sunk in the ground for the winter and if you have a patch of ground that is the simple answer. Or they can be wintered outside if the pots are packed round with insulating material. (Cheap and effective insulation is

SMALL TRIANGULAR PARTIALLY-WALLED GARDEN

(1) Family Tree: Apple, 3 varieties

(2) and (3) Fan-trained fruit trees on south-facing wall

(4) Mixed Herb Border

(5) Border with 2 ft. matted row of strawberries suitable for 'cloching'.

(6) and (7) Loganberries on posts and wire screening veg. and salad bed, behind.

(8) Flower border.

(9) Triangular patch of veg. and salad ground, rows running left to right and visible through or over screen.

(10) Paling or other fairly low type of fence with wide border of decorative veg. — sweet corn, Globe artichokes, etc.

MAINLY PAVED COURTYARD

(1) Window-box planted with herbs

(2) Single-cordon fruit trees framing window

(3) and (4) Plant troughs along edge of raised path, some with lettuce and other salads, others with short-growing half-hardy annuals.

(5) Two-tier plant stand against wall carrying tomatoes in pots

(6) Grape vine trained along top of wall.

(7) Fan-trained peach

(8) Table and chairs in foreground

(9) and (10) Fruit trees in pots

Obviously things ought to be in full growth and not dormant, as here.

provided by lightly crumpled newspaper in large polythene bags; bags which have held compost or peat are excellent, but they must be bone dry when the paper is put in, only partially filling them, and be tightly tied to prevent the contents getting damp.)

Trees in blossom may be taken under cover when night frost is threatened provided they are stood out again in the daytime.

Pot-grown trees are in bush form on dwarfing stocks. Kinds available include apples, plums, pears, peaches and figs. The really adventurous will find some citrus fruits also for sale.

Detailed instructions will be supplied by the nurseryman, and these should be followed implicitly, especially in regard to re-potting and the type of potting compost used. Trees are sent out in compost containing long-lasting nutrients, and advice should be sought on the correct mixture to use in re-potting. This operation is not performed yearly as it once was; some years a bit of the compost is scraped away from the top and fresh added. Re-potting, however, does not harm or even check the trees if done carefully. Large, woody roots may be cut cleanly back to encourage the fibrous ones through which the tree feeds, and some soil may be shaken off without completely breaking up the root-ball. A larger size pot may be needed, but don't think you are doing the tree a kindness by putting it into one a lot bigger than the volume of its roots. Root restriction keeps the tree small and fruitful, and it may be years before it graduates from a 12 in. to a 16 or 18 in. pot or tub.

A space of about 1 sq. yd. per tree must be allowed on the standing ground, and the site should be as sunny and sheltered as possible. Shelter from wind is very important now that soil-less composts and plastic pots are being used—light to handle but decidedly top-heavy. If there is danger of trees blowing over the pots should be wedged between concrete blocks.

Choice of varieties will be partly determined by the question of pollination (see Chapter 2). Many of the best-known ones are available in pots, including Family Trees.

Culinary herbs were of great importance up to the end of the seventeenth century, largely because staple foods were dull or just plain bad. They are becoming important again now to serious cooks for equally good if not identical reasons.

Herbs should always be grown 'in or around the house', somewhere where a fresh sprig is snatchable in a quick dash from the kitchen. Some herbs are suitable for window-box culture, others only for larger containers or small beds. With a few exceptions they like a sunny position and a well-drained soil. JI potting composts are satisfactory for container growing, and the soil-less composts for annual herbs. Perennial varieties in soil-less composts may need re-potting annually. A good home-made mixture would be: ½ garden soil, ¼ peat or compost, ¼ coarse sand, and a sprinkle of JI base. Many herbs are easily raised from seed, especially, in my experience, thyme, sage, chervil, borage, basil, and marjoram. Where only a few are wanted, however, it is easier to buy plants—with the exception of parsley, which is always grown from seed.

A Selection of Useful Herbs. All can be grown in very small beds or in large containers like tubs, troughs or 12 in. pots. Those which are also suitable for window-box work are indicated by the letter 'W'.

Balm. Perennial. Plant in autumn or spring. Likes more moisture than most herbs. Height 3 ft. Stems cut for drying when flowers are open. Aromatic, lemon-flavoured leaves. Flavouring in soups, stews and, sparingly, in salads.

Bay. Sweet Bay. Shrub. Will grow to 20 ft. tree but often cut back by frost. Very suitable for tub in sheltered position. Water frequently in summer. Basis of *bouquet-garni.*

Bergamot. Hardy perennial. Decorative red flowers. Likes partial shade. Height 15 in. Leaves and flowers used in salads.

Borage. Annual, easily grown from seed. Blue flower. Height 18 in. Too large for the window-box when full-grown but could be given a place while small. Flavouring drinks, especially claret and iced drinks. Chopped leaves in salads and mixed with cress.

Chervil. W. Annual. Quick growing. Sow April or September. Finely-cut curled leaves and white flowers. Aniseed flavour. Flavouring for egg and fish dishes. Ingredient of 'fines herbes' in omelettes etc.

Chives. W. Perennial. Grows in clumps, propagated by division. Mauve flower, but should be cut right down on reaching flowering stage in summer to encourage new growth. Any sort of container outdoors, and can be potted up and kept on kitchen window-sill in winter. This should not be done until December, when the plant will have been dormant for a few weeks and will respond quickly to warmth. Compact habit, ideal for window-box. Delicate onion flavour. Use instead of spring onions.

Dill. Annual. An old English herb, both leaves and seeds used. Traditionally a flavouring for fish.

Fennel. Perennial, best grown as annual. Planted or sown March/April. Height up to 3 ft. Slight aniseed flavour. Fish sauces, salads, or seeds as flavouring in soup.

Garlic. Bulbous perennial. Propagated by planting individual bulblets ('cloves') 1 in. deep and 4 to 6 in. apart in March. Cloves multiply by division like shallots and are lifted end of July, dried in sun and hung up in bunches. Prefers light soil. Hardy, much cheaper to grow than to buy, but needs more space than is justified in window-box. Most powerfully scented and flavoured member of onion family. Regarded as valuable medicinally for some 3,000 years.

Marjoram. Pot Marjoram. Perennial. Propagated by root division in autumn. Height 2 ft. Meat, fish, stuffings and in *bouquet garni*.

Marjoram. Sweet Marjoram. W. Half-hardy annual. Could be sown in window-box in April and thinned to 6 in. Same uses as pot marjoram, but rather different spicey flavour.

Mint. W. Perennial. Propagated by root division spring or autumn. Likes good soil, full sun or partial shade, and plenty of water when growing. Top-dress with compost in autumn. Roots may be dug up about Christmas-time, packed into pots of soil-less compost and brought into house or greenhouse for early picking. Very suitable for window-box and much better used freshly picked. Spearmint (Mentha viridis or Mentha spicata) is best variety.

Parsley. W. Biennial, sown once or twice a year to ensure succession of young growth. Sow March and July, $\frac{1}{2}$ in. deep, and keep moist. Seed very slow germinating—often a month or more. Thin seedlings to at least 3 in. Any good soil but must not be deficient in lime. Will do in partial shade. Protection of cloche or sheltered corner a help in winter. Choose a compact variety, Dobies' Perfection, Green Gem, or Imperial Curled.

Rosemary. Evergreen shrub. Plant spring or autumn. Suitable for tub culture in sunny position. Fragrant foliage, bluish flowers. Slow-growing, height about 3 ft. Leaves a powerful flavouring used with veal and chicken. Decorative and loaded with legend.

Sage. Semi-prostrate shrub. Raised from seed sown in April or cuttings in sandy compost in May. Not long-lived, becoming straggly and dying out. Keep pruned back to encourage young growth. Likes full sun and sheltered position. Often winter-killed in rural areas, but better survival rate in towns. Leaves can be dried and stored in jars. Meat dishes and stuffings.

Thyme. W. Dwarf shrubby perennial. Propagated by division in spring or from seed. Sandy soil and full sun. Quite happy in cracks between paving stones. Nice window-box edging. Common thyme (Thymus vulgaris) is the chief culinary species, but the Lemon Thyme (Thymus citriodorus) is also used and can be got with gold or silver variegated foliage. Thymus fragrantissimus is orange scented, and the Corsican Thymus herba-barona is a prostrate variety with a caraway scent. Thyme shoots can be picked and dried when flowering. Used in many ways and another *bouquet-garni* essential.

All herbs mentioned, with the exception of parsley, can be obtained as plants from Laxton and Bunyard, who also supply complete collections. Ask for leaflet 'Herbs and Aromatic Plants'.

A wide selection of herb seeds is quoted in Sutton's catalogue, including an easily grown and reasonably priced collection.

MUSHROOMS

The mushroom has become an important part of the menu, and its distinctive flavour elevates many an otherwise hum-drum dish. Increasingly it appears, raw and thinly sliced, in salads.

We have been well served by the commercial mushroom growers, prices have fallen over the years and supplies are plentiful. But home-grown mushrooms may be cheaper still, costing as little as 5p a lb. They can be grown literally anywhere; outdoors in any outbuilding, or indoors in attic or cellar. Of all edible crops they are the only one which can be grown from start to finish in full light, partial light, or total darkness, with no effect on yield.

There seems no reason why mushrooms should not be a regular amateur product, and they are a peculiarly fascinating subject for any gardener.

The Compost. The word has turned up again, in another slightly different context. Mushroom compost is something special, and at one time was made only from fresh horse manure. This is now impracticable for the town gardener, and horse manure is such a rarity that substitutes have had to be found. In amateur hands they are probably more reliable than the real thing.

The 'body' of the mushroom, the mycelium, consists of white mould-like threads spreading through and feeding upon the compost. The mushroom that we eat is merely the reproductive part of the plant, pushed above the ground to produce spores. The number of mushrooms produced depends on the vigour of the mycelium and the quality of its nourishment in the compost.

The basis of the compost is straw, with the actual horse droppings functioning as an activator in the traditional mixture. The modern forms still use either straw or straw chaff, but with a different form of activator.

The obtaining of straw has been touched on in Chapter 1, but for mushroom compost the best plan is to buy a large bag of wheat straw chaff from a corn merchant. This is much tidier and easier to handle than straw. Suppliers of the special activators and of the mushroom spawn which is sown in the prepared compost are listed in Appendix 1. Enough spawn and activator for 50 sq. ft. of bed costs about £2, and crops of 1 lb. per sq. ft. are not uncommon.

Methods of preparing the compost vary according to the brand of activator used, but all are simple and detailed instructions on spawning and management are provided. Apart for the compost, the only other material used is a little soil for 'casing' the beds—covering the tops. The prepared compost is perfectly inoffensive and boxes of mushrooms may be grown anywhere in the house where room can be found; the

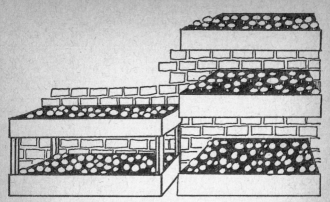

Mushroom beds on shady side of wall enclosed by boards.
Should be roofed with tin or plastic to keep rain off

only smell is the typical rather attractive mushroom odour.
Once the beds or boxes are spawned the only attention needed
is regular light watering. This must never be heavy enough to
soak the compost, so that no question of drips or drainage
will arise. Cropping begins about eight weeks after spawning
and may continue for two or three months, though it is not
continuous, the mushrooms coming in 'flushes'. They are not
cut, but are twisted gently out of the casing soil, the stems
being trimmed afterwards.

Growing Conditions. The best temperature is between 50 and
60°F., and this means that spring and autumn are the best
seasons for growing outdoors or in an unheated shed. In
cellar or attic, or anywhere that can be kept at room temperature, successional crops can be grown all the year round. The
temperature limits are not of course absolute, I have known
mushroom beds to be frozen and to continue in production
when they warmed up. Summer warmth will not hurt for a
time, but for maximum results a steady 'autumn day' temperature is the natural thing.

Mushroom beds are made 6 in. deep, and wooden boxes or
trays of that depth can be arranged in the ways illustrated.
Outdoors, a surround of 6 in. board can be made, a good place
being against the shady side of a wall. An outdoor bed should
be roofed with tin or plastic to keep rain off and permit
controlled watering.

MUSTARD AND CRESS

The stuff sold under this name has no cress in it and is not even true mustard. It is the coarser rape, the seed of which is cheaper and often used for green manuring.

Cress, once known as 'tea-cress' from its general use in sandwiches, is altogether more tender and better flavoured than the long-stemmed stuff that you buy, and mustard and cress together are a natural pair like eggs and bacon or fish and chips.

A shallow plastic seed tray is the handiest thing for growing m-&-c. indoors. One without drainage holes is less likely to make a mess, but with this you must be very careful not to over-water and leave everything floating.

Seed can be sown on a thick pad of folded Kleenex, but I prefer an inch of soil or soil-less compost. Make the surface firm and level, damp it thoroughly, and sprinkle the seed thickly over it. Press it down gently with the backs of the fingers but don't cover it with soil or compost. When sown the seed should be about an inch below the rim of the tray which is then covered with cardboard or brown paper.

One might as well sow the mustard and cress at the same time, ignoring the advice to sow the cress anything from one to four days earlier. Individual batches of seed vary so much in germinating time that this is just as likely to have both at the cutting stage simultaneously.

Keep the covered tray in a warm place but not in a hot airing cupboard. Glance at it daily and water when necessary. Once germinated, the seed-leaves shoot up very quickly and when they reach the paper cover it must be removed and the tray stood on a light window-sill for them to turn green. Time: about ten days from sowing to cutting.

White Mustard and Triple Curled Cress are the right varieties, and should be bought by the ounce and not in small packets.

SALADS IN CONTAINERS

Salads in window-boxes are nothing new but results are not always satisfying. Choosing the right things to grow is all-important within the limitations of container gardening. For instance, four large hearting lettuce will almost fill a 3 ft. box or trough, and once cut the cupboard is bare. But five or six loose-leaf Salad Bowl lettuce in the same space will provide crisp leaves for weeks on end. One cannot make the best use of these very limited resources by trying to grow a bit of everything normally grown in the garden.

Whether you have window-boxes, or pots and tubs, you will profit by concentrating on: (1) Green salads that furnish successive pickings of leaves. (2) Tomatoes. (3) Substitutes for spring onions. Varieties suggested will all do well in JI Potting compost or a similar home-made mixture, but a proportion of fresh soil must be added annually to boxes used for small salads, and tomatoes will of course always be potted up in new compost.

Green Salads. Lettuce Salad Bowl can be sown in March/April. If they are to be the only crop in the box, sprinkle the seed thinly over the surface and cover with ½ in. of compost. Thin out and use the thinnings as they grow, leaving the plants 6 to 8 in. apart. Remove the outer leaves as required. Even in a full-sized garden this lettuce is worth growing for the quality of its curly leaves in dry weather. It also has the advantage of remaining a 'good-looking' plant if care is taken over the leaf-gathering.

Lambs Lettuce or corn salad is described in Chapter 4. Grown in a sheltered window-box or trough it is the winter equivalent of the loose-leaf lettuce and in a good compost and kept fairly moist is a productive little plant. Sow broadcast in late summer and thin out to 4 in. all round.

Sorrel is often listed among the herbs but seldom as a vegetable or salad. It was at one time a quite important crop commercially, and Mr. John Organ, in his book *Rare Vegetables*, specifically recommends it for summer salads. The variety grown is the French or Broad Leaved, which you will find in most catalogues. It is a perennial, but if allowed to grow on for a second year becomes too big for a window-box and tends to develop a bitter flavour. It is best treated as an annual, sown in March and used as the leaves become worth picking. One of its useful features is that it will grow in complete shade.

American Land Cress (see Chapter 4) can be grown for winter salading in large pots or tubs, but is hardly worth the trouble when a succession of mustard and cress is so easily produced indoors.

Tomatoes. The standard tall-growing tomatoes can be grown outdoors in pots exactly as described in Chapter 4. The only difference to growing in the open ground is that the container-grown ones may have the advantage of a slightly longer season and consequently an extra truss of fruit. In a sheltered yard or balcony it should be possible to plant them up in early May. If the pots are stood against a wall light covering such as an old dust-sheet can be suspended in front of them on cold nights after planting and again when fruit is ripening in autumn.

Plastic or clay pots or small tubs can be used, but a 10 in. pot is about the minimum size for these tall varieties. JI Potting is probably the best compost but a soil-less type may be used if regular liquid feeds are given after the fruit is set. Fill the pot two-thirds full for planting and add more compost when the roots appear on the top.

Watering is a considerable problem with pot-grown toms. which may need attention more than once a day. When only morning and evening watering is possible it is safest to stand the pots in a trough of moist peat—and this applies to other large plants in pots which have to be left on hot summer days. Many preventable tragedies occur from neglect of this simple precaution. The peat need only be 5 in. deep, 2 in. under the pots and the rest packed closely round the sides. With tomatoes the drainage hole should be left open for the roots to escape into the peat—a modified form of the ring culture described in the previous chapter. A mat of roots soon forms under the pot and if the peat is always watered at the same time as the compost the plant has a reserve to draw upon.

The tomatoes must be supported as they grow and a bamboo stuck in the pot is usually inadequate when the trusses get heavy. If backed by a wall strings can be attached about 3 ft. up and the plants trained up them as in the greenhouse.

Window-box Varieties. Amateur Improved, Atom or Primabel produce normal-size fruits and being of dwarf, spreading habit don't look outlandish in a window-box. But really for this purpose I prefer the small-fruiting kinds like Tiny Tim which I have fruited in 4 in. pots. A newer version is the American F_1 hybrid Small Fry, which has slightly larger fruit. Dobies' Sugarplum is very suitable for pots on a plant stand, for its small, sweet-flavoured fruit hang in long

pendulous trusses. Incidentally, the quality of all these miniature varieties is first class.

A major deterrent to the growing of out-of-the-ordinary
tomatoes, whether the tinies or the superbly flavoured large
Continental types, is the difficulty of buying plants. It's
odds-on that only Moneymaker or something equally ordinary
will be available and that anything else must be grown from
seed. If you have no greenhouse the alternatives are: (1) Ask
the seedsman advertising the variety if he knows where
plants are obtainable. (2) Buy the seed and persuade a friend
who *has* got a greenhouse to raise plants for you on a share
basis. (3) Grow them yourself on the window-sill. This is
quite practicable, especially with one of the little indoor
propagating cases which are now so popular for raising house
plants.

Green Onions. Chives, which we have included among the
herbs, are the first choice. They have a non-productive
period in the winter, however, and such salad onions as are
on the market at this time are often dear and of poor quality.
The home-grown alternatives are welsh onions and scallions.

Welsh Onions in the garden are referred to in Chapter 4.
They are equally hardy and useful in pots or window-boxes,
remaining green in hard weather and easily increased by
splitting the clumps in spring. Firms selling herb plants can
usually supply them.

Scallions are an old gardener's method of using surplus
onions at the end of the winter. The bulbs, often sprouting
and too soft for kitchen use, are planted out to yield green
shoots long before the spring sown salad onions are ready.
Indoors, scallions are produced very quickly; use ordinary
bulb onions from the greengrocer—the smaller, scruffier and
cheaper the better—and plant them in peat, compost or bulb
fibre in shallow pots. Pack them in as tightly as possible with
an inch of compost below them and the same above to ensure
a length of white stem. Keep watered and in ordinary room
temperature. The growth is paler and more tender if not exposed to full light. A batch which I planted up on January
15th, showing no sign of shooting, had made 5 in. of growth
in ten days.

THE STRAWBERRY BARREL

Looking through some publications to find out when and where this subject has been mentioned I found it in *Gardening for Beginners* (1899) as a 'new and novel way of growing the Strawberry', and in a 1971 American magazine as an exciting new decoration for patio or terrace. It was probably easier to set up in 1899 because at least one firm was then selling ready-prepared barrels; now it seems to be a D.I.Y. job.*

Preparing the Barrel. First catch your barrel, and frankly I can't help you. There are still lots of wooden casks about, though, and enquiries at the pub, grocer's, greengrocer's, or junk dealer's will eventually locate one. You could use a plastic water butt and make the necessary holes in it with an electric soldering iron, but this would be expensive and not as nice to look at as the genuine article.

Any size barrel from 10 to 50 gallons will do, but since the object of the exercise is to plant up the sides of the barrel and not merely the top a bigger barrel means a bigger strawberry bed.

Wash out the interior of the barrel thoroughly and paint it with a harmless preservative such as Cuprinol. The outside may be painted or left in its natural state. If the staves seem to be working loose in the hoops the barrel should be stood in a shady place and repeatedly dowsed with water until they are tight again. Otherwise it may fall to pieces when you begin operation.

Bore a few 1 in. drainage holes in the bottom. Then draw chalk lines round the circumference, the first a foot from the ground, the others at 8 or 9 in. intervals. Equal spacing is not important but the circles must be well clear of the hoops. The last one should be about 9 in. from the top.

Now bore 2 in. diameter holes every 9 in. round the circles in staggered formation, each hole coming midway between the pair above and below it. Several types of power tools are suited to the job and extreme neatness is not vital because the holes will be invisible.

Filling and Planting. The two operations are performed simultaneously and enough soil to fill the barrel must be ready when the plants arrive. A mixture of two-thirds soil, one-third peat plus 14 lb. of coarse sand, 1 lb. of JI base,

*Ready prepared ones *can* be bought again. See 'Suppliers', p.146.

and 1 lb. of fine bone meal to the barrelful will last for several years. To buy enough made-up compost would be costly and if you have no garden you will probably have to cadge some soil from a friend who has or perhaps from a nearby building site.

You also need some drainage material, stones, broken crockery and other oddments you want to get rid of. Finally,

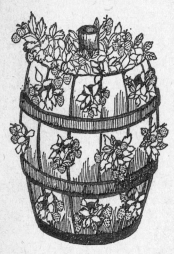

Strawberry Barrel. Note water pipe through middle.

you want a length of wide-bore piping; rainwater downpipe is ideal and if secondhand and rusty no matter. Seal one end by hammering it flat and punch it so full of holes that it looks like an elongated sieve. It should be a little longer than the height of the barrel.

Site the barrel carefully, remembering that it will be too heavy to move. A sunny, sheltered place is desirable, but some shade doesn't matter. Nor does the fact that one side of the barrel may get almost no sun—the berries will just be slower ripening. Stand it on bricks or 4 by 3 in. wood blocks.

Put the drainage layer in, then enough soil to bring the level up to the first row of holes. Pack this down solidly so that it doesn't sink later. Push the sealed end of your punctured pipe into this layer so that it stands vertically in the centre of the barrel.

Insert the roots of the plants through the holes, spreading them out and holding them in place with a little soil. When the circle is complete fill in with soil up to the level of the next lot of holes, make solid and water thoroughly. Repeat the cycle up to the top, where another three or four plants are put in around the projecting end of the pipe.

Watering a deep mass of soil is always tricky, and strawberries must not be allowed to get dry at the roots. By repeatedly filling up the central pipe all levels are moistened by seepage; overhead watering alone can result in a bog at the top and drought below. If any feeding is neccessary a liquid organic can be given.

Planting is best done in early autumn. Frost will not harm established plants; barrel grown-strawberries have survived spells with temperatures down to 8°F.

Most runners should be removed. Occasionally one may be tucked into a hole where a plant has died to form a replacement.

Varieties. One of the perpetuals (see Chapter 2) should be chosen. Their much longer season and heavier crop than the June-fruiting types dictate this. They cannot be replanted annually, as suggested, but under these conditions they don't get too rumbustious. St. Claude, with its dark green foliage and compact habit, is a good choice.

Slugs can't get at 'barrelled' strawberries, and birds too are said to leave them alone. (I have my doubts and would always be prepared to make a circular cage of 1 in. mesh wire netting.)

WINDOW-BOX STRAWBERRIES

I have grown perpetuals in many sorts of containers and have no doubt that they would do well in a window-box. Edward Hyams, in his strawberry classic mentioned previously, thinks them entitled to a place there for the sheer beauty of the plant when its fine foliage, white flowers and red berries are seen at close quarters.

A further point is that as the perpetuals are late starting into growth they can be interplanted with the smaller spring bulbs such as scillas, crocus, and chionodoxas, which will have finished before the strawberries overshadow them.

JI Potting No. 3 with the addition of a little extra peat is a good growing medium and a peat mulch should be given in spring.

Any perpetual variety will do, but an expansive one like Sans Rivale will need very few plants to fill a large box.

APPENDIX I
Suppliers

APPENDIX II
Books and Pamphlets

APPENDIX III
Organizations

Suppliers

Firms listed are either those with whom I have had dealings or are nationally known.

Many requirements may be bought locally, but anything out of the ordinary is often difficult to find. Suppliers of the specialized or unusual are therefore noted.

SEEDS IN GENERAL

Carters Ltd., Raynes Park, London, SW20.
Dobie & Son, Ltd., Chester.
Hurst Ltd., Witham, Essex.
Suttons Seeds, Reading. London shop: 161, New Bond St., W1.
Thompson & Morgan, London Rd., Ipswich, Suffolk.

UNUSUAL VEGETABLES

Dobie's: Ask for leaflet *Vegetables for Epicures*.
Carters: Ask for George B. Roberts' specialities.
Most varieties suggested are supplied by all the above firms. Celtuce, and outdoor cucumber Burpless are at the time of writing listed only by Thompson & Morgan.

FRUIT

Laxton & Bunyard, Brampton, Huntingdon, PE18 8NE.
Rivers Nurseries, Sawbridgeworth, Herts.
Seabrooks, Boreham, Chelmsford, Essex.
Blackmoor Nurseries, Blackmoor, Liss, Hants.
L. & J. Howard, Daymens Hill Nurseries, Maldon, Essex. (For organically grown strawberries).
Viticultural Research Station, Oxted, Surrey. (Grape vines).

SPECIALIZED FRUIT ITEMS

Family Trees: Laxton & Bunyard.
Fruit trees in Pots: Rivers.
Cordon and Fan-trained Trees: Most fruit nurseries.
Cordon Soft Fruits: Several of the above, especially Rivers.
Standard Gooseberries: R. Hill, Appleton, Abingdon, Berkshire.
Grape Vines: Apart from the Viticultural Research Station, many general nurserymen stock them. Rivers have a large selection for both greenhouse and open-air culture. Laxton & Bunyard stock The Cambridge, recommended for outdoor growing.

HERBS

Herb Seeds: Nearly all seedsmen sell them as individual varieties or in collections. Suttons have a collection of six annual varieties. Carters' collection of ten varieties comes with a booklet on herb growing by Edward Hyams and 20 cookery cards by Robert Carrier.
Herb Plants. The Old Rectory Herb Garden, Ightham, Kent. Laxton & Bunyard. Evetts, Ashfields Herb Nursery, Hinstock, Market Drayton, Salop. Kent Country Nurseries, Challock, Ashford, Kent (especially for all varieties of mint). For London shoppers: Justin de Blank, Elizabeth Street, SW1.

SUNDRIES

If unable to find what you want locally, try: E. J. Woodman & Sons, High St., Pinner, Middlesex. (24-hour phone service).
Peat, Compost, Organic Fertilizers: P. Garford Ltd., Walpole St. Andrew, Wisbech, Cambs. Maskells, 2, Stephenson St., London, E16. Deliveries in large or small quantities.
Window-boxes and Other Containers: A variety of wood, plastic, and fibre-glass boxes and tubs is available at all garden centres, and will be found in Woodman's catalogue. London shoppers will find extra-deep boxes at Rassell, 80, Earls Court Rd., W8.
Strawberry Barrels: R. Ward Ltd., Milkwall Station, Coleford, Glos. Barrelhouse, Beacon Drive, St. Agnes, Cornwall. Both firms supply a wide-range of plant tubs.

Pots and Tomato Rings: Available everywhere. A particularly interesting range of plastic pots, seed trays and sets of tomato-growing equipment for the amateur is supplied by Molewood Plastics, 58, Duncombe Rd., Hertford, Herts.

Reinforced Plastic Sheeting: Flexipane Ltd., Priory Works, The Street, Newton St. Faith, Norwich. Flexipane is a heavy wire-reinforced polythene, obtainable made up into cloches or in rolls. It appears to be a very suitable material for glazing the protective frames for wall fruit described in Chapter 2, or for making inexpensive unbreakable lights for ordinary garden frames. Sample on request from manufacturers.

Ordinary Polythene Sheeting, Bags, Plastic Bird-netting: Trans-atlantic Plastics Ltd., Garden Estate, Ventnor, I.O.W. and about 20 shops in southern England. Ask for Buyers' Guide.

Soil-testing Kits: A kit enabling the amateur to test for lime and also for NPK is obtainable from Sudbury Technical Products Ltd., 15, Honley Rd., London SE6., or from Boots. Attempts to correct soil deficiencies on the basis of NPK readings, however, is not advised. Better to maintain a steady build-up of the soil's organic content and to confine testing to checks on the pH, in case lime is needed. A simple lime-testing outfit made by Murphy provides for eight tests. Available at most garden shops or from Woodmans.

Mushroom Spawn and Compost-makers: Pure culture spawn and composting material 'Boost' in small quantities from Dobies. Also: B.M.I. Products, 420, London Rd., Mitcham, Surrey, for rather larger quantities of materials and detailed instructions.

GREENHOUSES

Here one can only suggest a few well-known manufacturers whose catalogues will be helpful in assessing the relative prices of different types.

Edenlite Ltd., Station Lane, Witney, Oxfordshire, and Crittall-Hope Ltd., Horticultural Dept., Braintree, Essex, both specialize in aluminium alloy construction. Putty-less glazing, all modern refinements, and the higher price range. Banbury Buildings Ltd., Ironstone Works, Banbury, Oxfordshire, and showgrounds from Glasgow to Southampton. Both wood and metal construction, but specializing in high quality cedarwood.

Worth Buildings Ltd., Telford, Shropshire. The 'Oakworth'

and 'Cedarworth' ranges are more top-quality timber jobs—
I know of a smallish 'Oakworth' erected in a very exposed
position nearly 25 years ago which is still going strong. Park
Lines & Co., 717/719, Seven Sisters Rd., London, N15, and
T. Bath & Co., Tonbridge, Kent, come within the moderate
price bracket for timber construction.

GREENHOUSE HEATERS

Electric Fan heaters, Propagators, Soil-warming Cables: Autogrow
Ltd., Quay Rd., Blyth, Northumberland; Humex Ltd., 5,
High Rd., Byfleet, Surrey. Humex also market a simple and
versatile automatic watering system for those whose greenhouse plants must be left all day.

Paraffin Heaters: Aladdin blue-flame heaters are available
through all garden stores. I can vouch for their extreme
reliability, and they can now be fitted with automatic feed
tanks to eliminate the chore of daily filling. Eltex heaters are
also generally on sale, and the new models are much in
advance of those which I have used successfully in the past.
If you want to maintain a rather higher temperature than is
possible with these comparatively small types, get a catalogue
from P. J. Bryant, Forest Rd., Fishponds, Bristol.

Books and Pamphlets

The following books should all be obtainable from your public library.

Fresh Food from Small Gardens, by Brian Furner. Stuart & Watkins.

The Complete Vegetable Grower, by W. E. Shewell-Cooper. Faber.

The Gourmet's Garden, by Douglas Bartrum. Faber.

Rare Vegetables for Garden and Table, by John Organ. Faber.

Fruit Growing, by N. B. Bagenal. Ward Lock.

Strawberry Growing Complete, by Edward Hyams. Faber.

Grapes Under Cloches, by Edward Hyams. Faber.

Some useful paperbacks would include the following from the Pan Piper 'Small Garden' series, though they may not all be in print at any one time.

The Small Garden, by C. E. Lucas Phillips.

Fruit for Small Gardens, by Howard H. Crane.

The Kitchen Garden, by Brian Furner.

Window-box Gardening, by Xenia Field.

Gardening in the North, by Kenneth Lemmon.

Gardening for the Elderly and Handicapped, by Leslie Snooks.

A comprehensive series of pamphlets and booklets on organic gardening is published by The Soil Association and The Henry Doubleday Research Association (addresses below). These are obtainable quite cheaply by post, and a list of those in print is supplied by The Soil Association. Particularly useful and interesting are:

Fertility Without Fertilizers

Compost, Comfrey and Green-Manures

Pest Control Without Poisons

All by Lawrence D. Hills.

Compost Making Q.R. Method, by Maye Bruce.

Organic Cultivation, by Richard Whittaker.

Functions of Humus and Compost, by R. F. Milton.

Take a Fresh Look at Food, by Margaret Hugh-Jones.

From The Royal Horticultural Society come two publications of great help to the beginner:
The Fruit Garden Displayed, and
The Vegetable Garden Displayed.
Both available by post at very reasonable prices.

Organizations

The Royal Horticultural Society, Vincent Square, London, SW1. Fellowship subscription either £3 or £5 per year. Admission to shows, to the gardens at Wisley, use of the library, the monthly Journal, and advice on horticultural problems are covered by the subscription. Fellows are also entitled to such services as soil analysis and the identification of fruit at moderate fees.

The Soil Association, New Bells Farm, Haughley, Stow-market, Suffolk. Subscription £3 per year. Large scale research in organic farming and gardening, and collection and publication on international basis of information on all related subjects. Individual advice and up-to-date quarterly Journal. An important source of publications on the really practical issues of our food and environment. The Henry Doubleday Research Association, Bocking, Braintree, Essex. Annual subscription, £2. Similar aims to those of The Soil Association, but much concerned with encouraging organic practice and research among private gardeners.

Index

Index

Herbs for Health and Beauty

SUZANNE BEEDELL

Herbs, properly prepared, mean health and beauty and here
you will find over 200 varieties carefully detailed and
described with full instructions for their use.

The major part of the book is devoted to the cosmetic and
medicinal use of herbs, but there are sections on their
preparation, where to find them and how to grow them.
With a detailed index for easy reference, HERBS FOR
HEALTH AND BEAUTY is a vital book for anyone
concerned with natural health and beauty.

A Sphere Book   40p

Easy Yoga Exercises

WILLIAM ZORN

The ancient science of yoga is an ideal – and surprisingly easy – way to improve health and natural beauty. William Zorn has compiled a series of exercises specially selected for beginners who will be able to follow his clear instructions without tying themselves into knots.

He has included a chapter on diet that will appeal to anyone seeking to lose weight and stay healthy.

All the simpler techniques are presented with photographs and drawings that make each exercise easy to follow.

A Sphere Book   30p

The Tomb of Tutankhamen

HOWARD CARTER

Tutankhamen's tomb, discovered in 1922 is an archaeological landmark. The tomb of the boy-king had lain unmolested by graverobbers for more than three thousand years, and it yielded a treasure of unimagined magnificence.

The story of the discovery is told by Howard Carter, who led the work of excavation. Not only does he provide a brilliant portrait of an 18th Dynasty Pharaoh, but he also communicates the feeling of awe and excitement which spurred the explorers as the tomb revealed its extraordinary riches.

The text is complemented by Harry Burton's contemporary photographs, and a selection of more recent colour plates.

A Sphere Book   £1.50

All Sphere Books are available at your bookshop or
newsagent, or can be ordered from the following address:

Sphere Books, Cash Sales Department,
P.O. Box 11, Falmouth, Cornwall.

Please send cheque or postal order (no currency), and allow
5p per book to cover the cost of postage and packing
in U.K., 7p per copy overseas.